FOR Bill —
Great videos with your Vegas!

Sport Riding Techniques

Nick Ienatsch
NN '05

Sport Riding
Techniques

HOW TO DEVELOP REAL WORLD SKILLS FOR SPEED, SAFETY AND CONFIDENCE ON THE STREET AND TRACK

BY NICK IENATSCH
FOREWORD BY KENNY ROBERTS

DESIGN BY TOM MORGAN

DAVID BULL PUBLISHING

*Dedicated with love to my mom, the writer,
and my dad, the rider.*

Front cover photo: Brian Blades. Back cover photos: Top: Brian Blades; Bottom: Brian J. Nelson; Author photo: George Grass

Library of Congress Control Number: 2003100263

ISBN: 1 893618 07 2

David Bull Publishing, logo, and colophon are trademarks of David Bull Publishing, Inc.

Book and cover design: Tom Morgan, Blue Design, Portland, Maine
Printed in Korea
10 9 8 7 6 5 4 3
David Bull Publishing
4250 East Camelback Road
Suite K150
Phoenix, AZ 85018
602-852-9500
602-852-9503 (fax)
www.bullpublishing.com
www.ienatsch.com
Motorcycle Safety Foundation, www.msf-usa.org, 1-800-446-0227

WARNING:
Riding motorcycles is inherently dangerous and can result in serious injury or death. The author and the publisher disclaim any liability incurred in connection with the use of the techniques and concepts described in this book. Ride within your personal limits. Always wear a helmet and protective riding gear, and observe the speed limit.

Previous page: Modern motorcycles have amazing capabilities, but only when given proper inputs by the human holding the handlebars. The quicker you ride, the more important these inputs become, meaning that every rider benefits from ongoing improvement regardless of experience level. How good do you want to be?

Right: Nick Ienatsch on the Zero Gravity Yamaha TZ250 in Laguna Seca's Corkscrew. Racing at the front of the AMA 250GP field while editor of *Sport Rider* magazine helped develop the techniques necessary to enjoy the street and excel at the track. (Brian J. Nelson)

Following page: This book explores front and rear tire traction using an easily understood 100-point scale. Tire traction is finite, and the limits must be approached in consistent, incremental steps, whether trail-braking into a corner or accelerating off the apex. (Hector Cademartori)

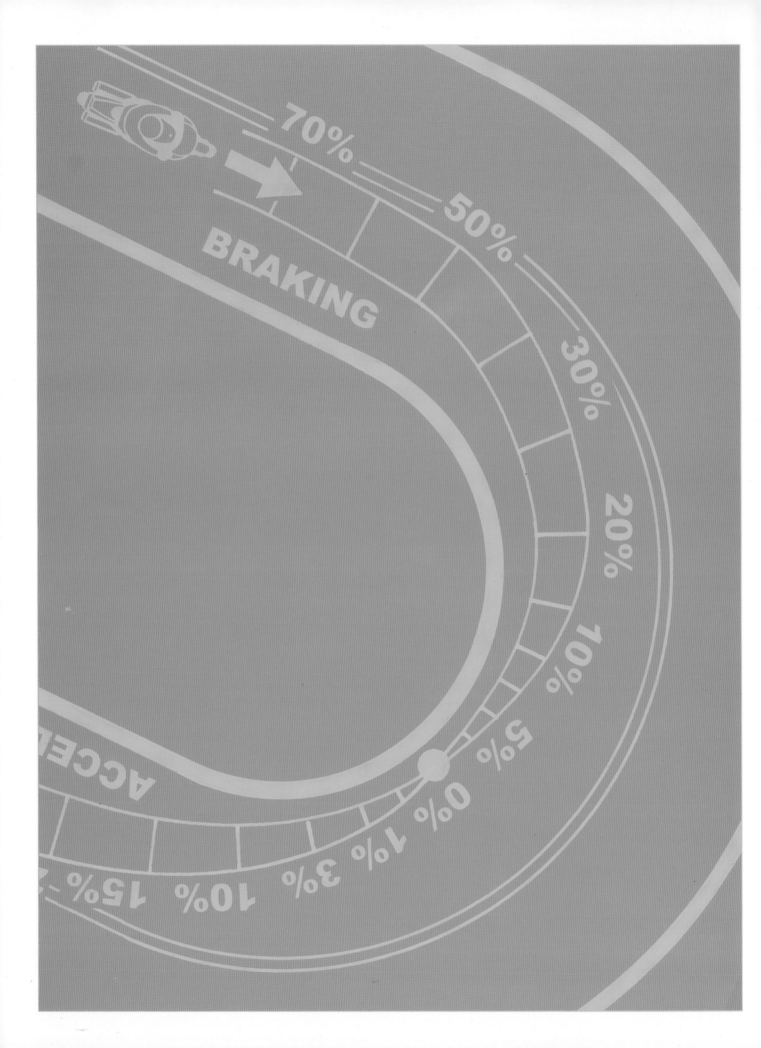

CONTENTS

ACKNOWLEDGMENTS

My first reaction is to thank everyone in the known world, simply because finishing my first book was a tremendous relief. If I acknowledge everyone who has helped me in my years as a motorcyclist (29 years and counting) the list would be ridiculously long but meaningful...to me. However, I've been instructed to keep the acknowledgments relative to the book. I'll try...

David Bull Publishing: Thanks for the great work of designer Tom Morgan and Anna Gilbert, and to Rachel Bernstein for her terrific editing. But the biggest thanks go to my friend, co-rider and publisher David Bull.

Photographers: We have a saying at the magazines, "No film, no story." Without the insightful work of the following shooters, there would be no book. A special thanks to ace photographers Brian J. Nelson, Brian Blades and Dennis Morrison. Thanks also to Jeff Allen, Dexter Ford, Patrick Gosling, Fran Kuhn, Gary Lehman, Jay McNally, George McQuiston, Tom Riles, Dennis Scully, and Marc Urbano. Great work, gentlemen.

Illustrator: A special thank you to Hector Cademartori, a motorcycle-riding illustrator who can take any complicated concept and draw it clearly and persuasively.

Cycle World and *Sportbike* magazine groups: These folks have been tremendous help, whether taking photos, riding in photos or helping in a hundred other ways. Thanks to super riders Don Canet and Mark Cernicky. Thanks also to David Edwards, Brian Catterson, Matthew Miles, Mark Hoyer, Jimmy Lewis, Robyn Davis, Brad Zerbel, Elaine Anderson, Paul Dean, Jason Colon, Ben Welch, Jason Black, Jim

Yeardly, Todd Egan and John Casimer. Great people, terrific publications. And David, I couldn't have done it without you!

Motorcyclist and *Sport Rider* magazine groups: I started this book while at *Sport Rider* and must thank the gang who got it all going in my head: Art Friedman, Mitch Boehm, Lance Holst, Jason Black, Siobhan Burns and Angela Barosso.

My racing partners: Racing taught me so much, mainly because I was free to focus on riding due to the extremely talented people supporting me. I'd like to thank everyone who helps me race, but will limit it to the group with whom I won club and national championships: Steve Biganski, Craig Erion, Kevin Erion, Steve Johnson, John Cordona, Dan Kyle, Glenn Cook, Dennis Smith, Jim Allen, Bob Graham, John Winslett, Tommy Lynch and Larry Pegram.

I have had a great deal of help with my riding/racing and I'd like to thank those who took the time to teach me so much: Keith Code, Eddie Lawson, Wayne Rainey, Thomas Stevens, my dirt-track coach Jeff Haney and, most of all, my riding-school boss, Freddie Spencer. I mentioned how much I continue to learn from Kenny Roberts' book, and I thank King Kenny for his words in the foreword.

I must thank my wonderful, wonderful parents, Ellie and Bill Ienatsch; my terrific wife, Judy, who inspires me, rides with me and keeps me constantly entertained; and the Lord Jesus Christ. And lastly, I thank you for reading this book and being my riding friends since my first day at *Motorcyclist* in 1984.

—Nick Ienatsch, January, 2003

Left: Successful national-level racing takes an enormous effort in time and money, but when things go well in practice you can have a laugh before the main event. Jon Cornwell (white helmet) and I (far left) are laughing at something Steve Biganski (standing directly behind the TZ) said—probably, "It was pretty good on Thursday, but I've tuned it to a standstill." (Brian J. Nelson)

FOREWORD

THE KEY TO DEVELOPING GOOD SKILLS IS PRACTICE, PRACTICE, PRACTICE

The guy who wrote this book has seen how hard the best riders work to get to the top and to stay on top. Team Roberts started a training camp in Spain to help European riders learn the basics of dirt track skills, which is largely an American sport. The camp in Spain was modeled on my California ranch, where Nick has trained with guys like Wayne Rainey, Eddie Lawson, John Kocinski and my kids, Kenny Jr. and Kurtis. The riding sessions we have are all playing, but there's a lot of learning taking place on these dirt bikes.

I first met Nick in 1990, when he came to the Ranch with Eddie Lawson, and he was just starting to race 250s. Journalists have always been a pain in the ass, so we beat him up pretty good on the motocross and dirt track. He didn't cry much. Junior was just starting to race 250s in WERA, so I was paying attention to the national scene, and noticed Nick finishing in the top three overall in AMA points a few times. He did OK on some four-stroke Hondas too. Not bad for a journalist.

But street riding is the focus of this book, and that involves more than just lap times. Most people can't even drive a car well, much less a bike, so *Sport Riding Techniques* should really help. I believe in rider training and riding technology at all levels, whether you're racing for the MotoGP world championship or just enjoying a weekend ride. I know Nick has been writing about riding technique in the magazines for years, and I wholly endorse this book. Anything that improves your riding and improves the acceptance of motorcycles is great with me.

Nick has mentioned how much my book, *Techniques of Motorcycle Roadracing,* helped his racing, and I hope this book helps your riding. This guy has worked hard on his riding and racing, and his book is the culmination of the attention he has paid to the techniques for success.

Left: Kenny Roberts was the first American 500 Grand Prix world champion, winning his first of three consecutive titles in 1978 for Yamaha. In his six years of GP battle, King Kenny won 22 500GP races and finished on the 500GP podium 39 times. He also won two 250GP races and finished on the 250GP podium five times. This quote sums up his outlook: "A major part of what makes a champion is determination. It's more important than natural talent, because there is so much that you can learn and work at." (Author's collection)

Above: Kenny the racer became Kenny the team owner, and Team Roberts won three 500GP world championships with Wayne Rainey. Kenny then broke away from Yamaha to build his own chassis and engine. For more on KR's team, visit www.teamkr.com. (Team Roberts)

SPORT RIDING TECHNIQUES

A BOOK IS BORN

Welcome to *Sport Riding Techniques,* a book devoted to high-performance motorcycle riding on the street and track. I add the term *track* because it's there that you can safely find the absolute limit of bike and rider, and several of the riding elements we'll discuss in this book are best suited to the track. However, street riding is what *Sport Riding Techniques* focuses on because street riding demands its own set of skills and issues its own challenges. Anyone who has ridden a motorcycle down a twisty road feels the addiction of this thrilling, satisfying and, if carelessly undertaken, potentially dangerous sport.

This book comes on the heels of a dozen articles I've written about the human side of the rider-bike equation for *Motorcyclist, Sport Rider, Sportbike* and *Cycle World* maga-

zines. Probably the most popular article I've written, "The Pace," describes and deals with developing the skills to enjoy your sport bike on the street while staying alive and out of jail. Several iterations of "The Pace" have appeared since the original in 1987, but I realized a book was needed not just to update "The Pace," but also to explore everything from urban survival to attending a track day. *Sport Riding Techniques* has almost nothing to do with the bike you ride. Instead, it's all about how you ride that bike.

On top of my magazine writing came work at riding schools, including former world champion Freddie Spencer's High Performance Riding School in Las Vegas. I began working for Freddie in 1997 as his lead instructor, and his lifelong racing experience opened my eyes to the techniques he mastered on the racetrack not just to win races, but to survive this difficult sport. As you will discover in this book, speed and safety aren't mutually exclusive. In fact, riding well is not only a great way to get around a racetrack at the lap record, but also a terrific way to become an old rider. Both are excellent goals.

Riding safely and within your limits takes focus, confidence, practice, patience and self-discipline. The approach I teach here and the skill exercises I recommend will help all riders appreciate the fact that there are serious techniques and guidelines for high-performance street riding. When a

Left: I've had some good success racing, finishing second in the 1995 AMA 250GP series. I'm shown here at Daytona in '96 with my new number plate. In '91, '93 and '94, I placed third overall in the 250GP championship, backed by Zero Gravity, Del Amo Yamaha, Dunlop, AGV and tuner Steve Biganski. (Brian J. Nelson)
Above: A cold, wet day at Suzuka found me aboard Mick Doohan's NSR500 for a look into the top echelon of motorcycling. As a writer for *Motorcyclist, Sport Rider, Cycle World* and *Sportbike,* I've ridden everything from the Britten to a 234 mph turbocharged GSX-R1340. Just so you know I'm completely hooked, I own more than 25 bikes . . . (Fran Kuhn, courtesy of *Motorcyclist*)
Right: Teaching at a riding school involves more than just riding well. The concepts to master techniques must be clearly explained and reinforced. I began teaching at riding schools in 1989 when I recognized that the increasingly sophisticated bike technology could best be enjoyed by improving riding technology. (Dennis Morrison)

rider like Freddie Spencer tells his students that the skills he is teaching them are the same skills he works on every lap, it becomes clear that proper riding techniques are for beginners and veterans alike. Motorcycles are designed to stop, turn and accelerate with certain inputs from the rider, and this book will refine your inputs while defining good riding.

USING THIS BOOK

Each chapter concludes with a section called Lessons from the Racetrack. In these sections, I explain how the information contained in the chapter applies to racing on the track, which is the purest example of our sport. At the track, only performance—determined by the stopwatch, finishing position and, at year's end, championship points—matters. I've always done well at the track, and many of the components of good street riding can be learned from racers. Just as Kevin Schwantz illustrated to me the importance of the rider's input, I hope Lessons from the Racetrack helps to keep you thinking about your street riding.

I also hope you use this book frequently as a reference. As your riding skills grow, rereading the information will spark you to new levels of safety and speed because your newfound skills will allow you to grasp a technique that was unavailable to you earlier. I hope nobody reads this book from cover to cover and then sets it permanently on the bookshelf, because there is simply too much to this demanding sport to grasp in one sitting. I still pore over *Techniques of Motorcycle Roadracing,* an old book by Kenny Roberts and Peter Clifford, and I hope your copy of this book becomes just as wrinkled and faded from use, with plenty of notes in the margins.

Right: God bless John Britten, the brilliant creator of the neatest bike I've ever ridden. Owner Jim Hunter allowed me to race his V-twin at Daytona and Road Atlanta in 1994. Britten realized that while his innovative technology was trend setting, the bike had to perform on the racetrack. And it did. (Brian J. Nelson)

Above: AMA nationals were a ton of fun for me in the mid '90s because I pulled double-duty, racing 250GP and SuperTeams (I'm shown here on the Dutchman Racing Yamaha 1000). My three years of double-duty resulted in two national championships, two No. 2 plates and two No. 3 plates. Whether you're on a quarter-liter two-stroke or unlimited four-stroke, the principles put forth in this book apply. (John Flory)

Below: A long straight followed by a tight, blind, right-hand corner holds catastrophic consequences for a rider who can't control speed and direction. If you make a mistake in a right-hand corner you could drift into the opposite lane and get killed by oncoming traffic. Sport riding demands exceptional skills, good judgment and leaving a margin for error. (Brian Blades)

CHAPTER 1

THE CHAIN'S WEAK LINK

TO FIND THE TRUE TECHNICAL PROBLEM, YOU NEED TO LOOK IN THE MIRROR

Take a look at the performance figures of any modern street bike, most of which have sub–three-second zero-to-sixty times that beat the most potent supercars, and it's obvious that riding skill is being far outpaced by motorcycle technology. To find the weakest performance link in the rider-bike chain, look behind the handlebar to the rider—this is the link that needs strengthening. By understanding and improving your rider inputs, not only will you become a better rider, but every ride will become more enjoyable. When you get on the latest and greatest from Japan, Germany, Italy or America, it will behoove you to have some special skills.

My approach deals with more than the fundamentals of riding a motorcycle, because a rider's physical skill means nothing if his judgment is flawed. In other words, no mat-

Bikes continue to improve and tires get progressively better, but single-bike crashes remain a serious problem in our sport. Make sure your riding technology keeps pace with bike technology. (Jeff Allen)

Above: Proper bike control means that you are able to place your motorcycle within inches of your desired line through a heavenly section of road. The more you know about riding, the more enjoyable this road will be. (Jeff Allen)

Left: Yikes. Through his riding position, this guy is saying, "Write me a ticket!" Tucking in on the street should be used only to stay out of the hail, dodge a bird or attract police attention. The problems here include a low line of sight, a low profile for already-challenged car drivers and the fact that most riders who tuck in don't readjust their mirrors. (Brian Blades)

ter how well you're capable of riding at 100 mph, you'll find big trouble if you insist on riding at that speed in a school zone. It's not enough to know how to twist the throttle; you must have the judgment to know when and where to do it.

The rider is the greatest single factor in a motorcycle's performance. My most memorable proof of this came in 1985 at the WERA 24-hour race held at Willow Springs Raceway. Dennis Smith, who owned the performance shop Cycle Tune, asked me to ride a Billy Foster–prepped Yamaha FZ750, certainly one of the best machines of the day. Just before midnight, I found myself in the hot seat circulating at what my brain told me were super-fast speeds, scything through the darkness faster than any human could possibly go. About 10 minutes into my stint, a beaten and abused FJ600 slammed past me midway through Willow's infamous turn eight and disappeared into the distance. Before I pitted to hand off the Cycle Tune machine to our team's next rider, I was lapped again by the same berserk FJ, a bike clearly slower than our FZ and certainly more poorly prepared. Until that race, I thought horsepower and preparation would win the day. Kevin Schwantz proved me wrong.

The young Texan had been racing the FJ all year and was clearly at home with its strengths and shortcomings. Schwantz had adapted to what the FJ offered him as a race bike, and the bike and rider had melded—a process you'll understand when it happens to you. Though it may have made 30 fewer horsepower than the Cycle Tune FZ750 and it barely limped through tech inspection, the man behind the handlebar had that FJ figured out. Lucky for the Cycle Tune team, none of Schwantz's teammates could match his pace on the 600, and we went on to win the race. But the best thing I got out of the race was an understanding of how much rider skill adds to a motorcycle. It isn't the only ingredient, but it's certainly the most important.

ON-BOARD ENGINEER

As you digest this book, bike setup will become much less important. You will realize how your operation of the controls, the movement of your body and the use of your eyes affect the motorcycle. We riders are on-board engineers, able to transfer weight forward, rearward and to the inside or outside of the motorcycle. We choose engine rpm, and that affects not just acceleration and deceleration but lean angle and turn-in rate. A wiggling bike might not need a steering damper adjustment if the rider relaxes his grip at the handlebar. A bike that won't turn might not need more rear ride height once the rider loads the inside foot peg and closes the throttle. Technically sound riders can ride anything well, and if Kevin Schwantz had decided to whine about setup, he never would have risen to the rank of World Grand Prix Champion. To be blunt: Quit worrying about two clicks of rebound or "needing" a pipe and jetting for more horsepower. Work on your engineering skills to find your bike's best performance.

IT'S NOT ABOUT GUTS

Testosterone and sheer bravery receive too much emphasis in the motorcycling world. *No fear* might work for bungee jumping, but not for riding a motorcycle on the street. Technique and concentration deserve much more credit. Add to them intelligence, intuition and desire, and you'll begin to describe not just the fastest roadracers but the best street riders as well. While I can't teach intuitiveness, you'll be surprised at how a bit of knowledge translates into a large gain in riding ability. Just the fact that you are thinking about your riding will lead to significant improvement, which, as you'll discover, leads to greater enjoyment. After all, if you're going to do something, why not do it well?

Left: Finessing the throttle, front brake and clutch begins with your seating position. Imagine trying to type on a keyboard while doing push-ups and you'll understand how tough it is to ride smoothly without sitting on the bike in a relaxed position.
A. Sitting too far from the tank locks the elbows, and that means you lose front-end feel. This rider has scooted back on the seat, and those straight arms will make his steering inputs abrupt and his control inputs even worse. Straight arms often feed wobbles and weaves into the bike's chassis because the front tire isn't being allowed to respond to imperfections in the road.
B. Sitting up against the fuel tank puts the rider's belly against the tank and often straightens the back. As soon as the back goes straight, the arms do too. The inevitable results are a loss of front-end feel, abrupt inputs and a lack of smoothness. Riders who sit too close to the tank often find themselves locked in position, losing the ability to move their shoulders to help load the foot pegs or transfer weight forward and rearward.
C. Ideally, your crotch should be about one inch from the back of the tank, your back slightly rounded and your arms bent. In this sport, the keys to success are precise operation of your throttle and front brake lever and your ability to steer and shift, so relaxed hands are mandatory. Relaxed hands begin with your seating position. (Brian Blades)

Right: Kevin Schwantz's path to this factory Yoshimura Superbike was facilitated by his willingness to ride anything to its limits. This is Daytona in 1987. Schwantz went on to race in 500GP and won the championship in 1993. (Nick Ienatsch)

CHAPTER 2

THE BASICS: BRAKING AND STEERING

LEARNING TO STOP AND TURN IS A LIFELONG STUDY, BUT THESE BASICS ARE LIFESAVING

The foundation of good riding skills is a solid understanding of the basics of motorcycle handling: You've got to learn to brake, and you've got to learn to steer. These are basic survival skills that you should constantly practice. You'll realize this when a car unexpectedly turns left in front of you; your braking and steering skills will help you avoid an accident that would be unavoidable to a less-practiced rider. Now is the time to step up your performance of these two basic skills and to work them into your favorite recreational ride, commute or racetrack day.

Whether it's on the back roads of the Rocky Mountains or the back straight at Mid-Ohio Raceway, those who master the arts of braking and steering are the best riders. Your brakes are a controlling device, significantly more powerful than any other part of the motorcycle; when used correctly, brakes make the difference between riding the motorcycle and being taken for a ride. Braking efficiently is your way to precisely control cornering speed, control the horsepower of a modern sport bike and control your panic response in stressful situations. Familiarity with the brakes adds a huge amount of confidence to your personal riding portfolio. If you ride with a lack of confidence, look to your mastery of your bike's braking system for a boost.

ON THE BRAKES

How fast do you ride? Let's say you enjoy cruising between the cornfields at 85 mph on Sunday mornings, with an occasional blast up to 100 mph when it's safe to do so. Do you know *how much time* it takes you to stop from 100 mph? Do you know *how much distance* it takes you to stop from 100 mph? *Cycle World* magazine tests stopping distances from 60 mph, and at that speed, bikes average 120 feet—and that's with perfect pavement, warm tires and an expert rider on board. Do you practice full panic stops from the speeds you usually ride?

You should, because that's the speed you might be riding

Left: How's this for confidence in the brakes? The rider got to this point not by grabbing the front brake lever but by squeezing it progressively harder until the front tire locked, rotating the bike into a stoppie.
Right: Thirty cones and an empty parking lot create a practice zone for braking and steering. The evenly spaced cones allow a rider to gauge improvement, and improvement comes from less aggression and more smoothness. (Dennis Morrison)

when the cow steps over the broken fence and wanders into your lane. But evidence points to the fact that many riders are better at twisting the throttle than squeezing the binders because twisting is easy and stopping hard isn't. Stopping hard takes practice. Lots of it.

If you ride at 100 mph, practice stopping from 100 mph and make it part of your riding ritual. Pick a parking lot or deserted frontage road and discover what your brakes can do. Braking practice has been incorporated into my daily commutes because I'm constantly riding different bikes from the magazine garage. I wait until there's no traffic behind me and try the brakes, slowly squeezing them the first time, then really working them hard from higher speeds. I'm willing to bet that once you discover how much distance it takes to stop your bike from high speed, you'll be much more careful about where and when you speed.

Practicing your braking will put you in touch with your bike's ability to shed speed quickly, which is a valuable point of reference when you begin using your brakes for more subtle speed changes at corner entrances. You'll learn the importance of maximum deceleration in which the tires are howling and near lock-up, but it's also important to master the fine-touch applications of braking, especially for trail-braking and other more complicated techniques discussed later in this book. You *must* become comfortable with your brakes.

PRACTICE STOPS

Pick a clean, deserted stretch of pavement, wear your best riding gear and practice stopping. The goal is repeatable stops at the threshold of front and rear tire lock-up. Notice the weight transfer forward as the bike begins braking. The

front tire becomes the workhorse during heavy braking as the weight shifts to the front and the rear tire becomes lightly loaded. Long-wheelbase bikes will leave more weight on the rear tire, allowing the rear brake to be of more use.

1. Begin slowly and carefully by making a few easy stops.

2. Studies show the fastest, shortest stops come from using both brakes, yet some sport riders stay off the rear brake entirely due to their fear of lock-up or due to a mistaken belief that using the rear brake doesn't help. Remember, it's okay to use the rear brake, but don't abuse it. Some manufacturers make the rear brake entirely too strong and easy to lock, especially when the front brake is used hard and the fork springs are compressed, transferring much of the bike's weight forward onto the front tire. The rear tire is lightly loaded and it takes a light, practiced touch to avoid locking it.

3. Use two fingers, the index and middle fingers, on the front brake lever. The old days of fading brakes pinching your fingers against the bar are long gone, and a whole-hand grab is not only too much pressure for today's low-effort systems, but it also reduces your control of the throttle when blipping (revving) the engine on downshifts. (You'll learn more about blipping in chapter 6.)

4. Squeeze the front brake lever like you'd squeeze the trigger of a gun—never grab it. A grab will overwhelm the fork springs, bottoming the suspension and either skidding the front tire or lifting the rear tire. With practice, you can bring the front tire to the threshold of lock-up, at which point you'll hear a howl from the contact patch. When you're good, quickly locking the front tire will become a game. If you accidentally lock your front brake, release it immediately to get the tire turning again because the bike will very quickly wash out the front end and low-side.

5. Develop the habit of resting your fingers on the front brake lever anytime the throttle is not wide open. In other words, if you're cruising through town or decelerating for a corner, have your fingers covering the front brake lever to cut reaction time.

6. Experiment with rear brake pedal pressure. Don't jab at it; push it down gently until you hear the rear tire howl just before lock-up or feel the back end become squirmy. (Some tires are quiet and you just feel the back end slew.) Locking the rear brake for a short time isn't a problem and may be unavoidable, and I hope you have already experimented with this as part of your braking practice. A locked-up rear brake can be dealt with in two ways: Leave it locked and steer with the handlebar to keep the bike upright and straight, or immediately get off the brake to get the rear tire turning again. In a true emergency, you might not have the mental capacity to relieve rear brake pressure, so practice locking up the brake and steering. Hmmm...sounds like a great thing to try on a dirt bike first!

STEERING CLEAR

Explaining how to steer a motorcycle is often more confusing than simply discovering how to steer on your own. Anyone who can ride a bicycle is familiar with a single-track vehicle's peculiar handling characteristics. A few years back, someone coined the term "countersteering" to describe the actions involved in turning a moving two-wheeled vehicle: You push on the left handlebar to deflect the front wheel to the right, which forces the bicycle or motorcycle to fall to the left. Confused? Think of it in terms of simply pushing in the direction you want to go: To turn left, push left, or to turn right, push right. If you can ride a bicycle or motorcycle, you are countersteering already. A little countersteering awareness goes a long, long way to help a beginning rider steer a motorcycle efficiently, and when that rider is ready for more subtle ways to affect a motorcycle's direction, she will use countersteering along with several other techniques examined in chapter 4.

Once you wrap your mind around the basic countersteering principle—push the handlebar in the direction you want to go—you're open to the almost infinite variations possible

when steering a sport bike. Suddenly, quick steering isn't just a way to avoid an accident, it's the secret to precision sport riding. Like braking, steering skills can be endlessly polished with an attendant improvement in your riding ability.

As you begin experimenting with your steering inputs, you'll discover the bike's willingness to turn is directly related to the force at the handlebar. Push lightly, and the bike will slowly bend in the desired direction. Jab at the bar, and the bike will slam over. Try a quick lane change with a quick push on the bar, then try a slow lane change with steady, light pressure at the bar. With understanding comes better riding, and your confidence rises with your enjoyment.

The faster you go, the greater the gyroscopic effect of the tires, wheels, chain, discs, etc., which means it takes more effort to deflect them off their chosen path. Changing lanes at 65 mph will take more bar pressure than changing lanes at 35 mph, and not just to initiate the turn, but to recover

Above right: OK, so our photo model is overdoing it a bit, but he has selected a deserted back road to practice his stops, and he is wearing protective riding gear. Practice in private, and practice a lot. (Brian Blades)
Middle and below right: Same bike, same rider, same speed, but different control inputs to illustrate the throttle and brake's ability to transfer weight forward and rearward. Light acceleration extends the fork and loads the rear tire (top), while light braking collapses the fork and loads the front tire. The best riders transfer weight with smooth control inputs (bottom). (Dennis Morrison)

Above left top: Eager anticipation or fright? This sign indicates a fun, challenging road ahead for riders who are in control of their bike's speed and direction. But if you lack these basic skills, this sign means trouble. (Brian Blades)
Below left bottom: This rider's braking technique is so ingrained that he has time to look at the camera while rotating a Ducati on its nose. Practice the techniques described in this book during every minute of every ride, so when an emergency happens, your reactions are correct. (Fran Kuhn, courtesy of *Sport Rider*)

as well. Much of a chassis designer's effort goes toward developing proper steering feel, balancing stability against turning ability to give steering characteristics that fit the bike's intended purpose. But no matter what kind of bike you ride, perfecting your inputs at the handlebar will broaden your bike's range of abilities well beyond mere descriptions like "stable" or "quick turning." And when you get a good handle on the basics of countersteering, there are some advanced steering techniques that will add further control and confidence to your riding.

Top: The front brake lever must become your best pal. Constant and habitual practice is the key to developing good skills, but only if your technique is correct. Treat the brakes like a speed rheostat, not an on/off switch. Squeeze, don't grab. (Dennis Morrison)
Above: We caught this rider in the middle of the most common type of single-bike accident. It began with a rushed corner entrance followed by target fixation on the edge of the road and a panicked stab at the rear brake. Education and practice can overcome these problems. (Brian Blades)
Left: How much fun would these riders miss if they couldn't turn their bikes? Roads like this highlight your ability to steer a motorcycle, and those abilities begin (but don't end) at the handlebar. (Jeff Allen)

Right: Racing in 600 Supersport, the 2002 AMA Superbike champion Nicky Hayden and his fellow racers balance lean angle and brake pressure with the utmost precision. The basics of precisely controlling the speed and direction of your bike are necessary skills no matter where you ride. (Brian J. Nelson)

STEER AT THE HANDLEBAR

This entire book is aimed at getting the rider to work with the bike, so the countersteering push and pull will soon be supplemented by more subtle steering methods that work in conjunction with countersteering. But before diving into the advanced steering concepts in chapter 4, you need to master countersteering. Learn how to turn your bike with pressure at the bar.

This chapter on the basics—steering and braking—takes attention away from speed, style or suspension tweaking and directs that attention right at the rider, where it belongs. It's so easy to get carried away by the non-essential extras and completely forget that a moving motorcycle must be controlled by the brakes and steering system. If you are a new rider or know a new rider, make sure these basics are mastered before worrying about anything else. If you can't stop and steer, you shouldn't be riding.

LESSONS FROM THE RACETRACK

FEEL THE RHEOSTAT Brake feel is more important than outright braking power because racers will use their brakes deep into the corner when necessary. It's called *trail-braking* (trailing off the brakes as the bike leans into the corner) and we'll be working on that in chapter 6. Quit thinking that the brake lever is an on/off switch and treat it like a speed rheostat.

CLEAN THE DISCS Race teams use electrical contact cleaner and sometimes glass-bead brake discs to clear off pad debris imbedded in the surface.

LESS REAR BRAKE IS MORE A race bike's rear brake shouldn't lock up no matter how hard the rider stands on it. Modify your rear brake (remove pad material, limit brake lever travel, etc.) so that it can't lock up. And don't be misled: The best racers use their rear brakes consistently. Why else would Mick Doohan have fashioned a thumb-operated rear brake when he hurt his right leg?

CHANGE THE FLUID Racers change their bikes' brake fluid frequently because heat and moisture reduce the fluid's boiling point. Think about changing your brake fluid three times a year if you ride year-round. Never reuse clutch or brake fluid, and keep your brake fluid bottle tightly sealed.

CHAPTER 3

THE EYES HAVE IT

GET YOUR EYES UP AND SCANNING

We can all remember instances of target fixation when we've fastened our eyes onto an object that we've wanted to avoid—a pothole, a rock or a wet white line—and then run right over it, almost as if we're frozen at the handlebar. There are plenty of racing incidents where a trailing rider follows a crashing rider off the racetrack, even though the trailing rider could have easily made the corner. Or how about looking off to one side of the road as you're riding and finding yourself fading in the direction you're looking? These are all examples of target fixation, where your body and motorcycle follow your eyes. In sport riding, you need to reprogram your eyes to look at the world correctly and to focus on where you need to be. You need to look to the path

Left: Resist the urge to stare at the rider you're following, whether on the street or track. Your main focus must remain on where you want your bike to be and what obstacles you are approaching, while your peripheral vision and an occasional quick glance are used to maintain the other rider's position as you ride. (Brian Blades)

Below: If you fix your gaze on any single problem, you put yourself in jeopardy of missing other threatening situations. Move your eyes! Most of us don't move our eyes quickly enough. (Hector Cademartori)

Above right: The process of avoiding obstacles involves three steps that can easily be remembered using the Motorcycle Safety Foundation's excellent acronym: SEE. The S is for Search. Constantly move your eyes, scanning your riding environment for potential problems. The first E is for Evaluate. Are there potential problems around you? It's much easier to respond when you recognize a potential problem early, which is why good visual habits are so important. The final E is for Execute. Quickly and smoothly carry out your decision through the motorcycle's controls. (Hector Cademartori)

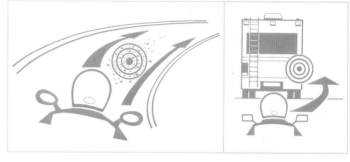

you want your bike to follow. Target fixation is okay—if you pick the right targets.

Visualize the proper line through corners and use your eyes to trace a path along the road and follow it. So when the car turns left in front of you, look to your escape route, not to the car's front bumper. When there's sand across the corner, look to the clearest path through it. If you're up in the mountains riding quickly, ignore the panoramic view and concentrate only on the road. Get tough with your eyes. Use them to look past a crashing rider, a beautiful view or a pothole. Use them to put your bike exactly where you want it to be.

Using your eyes correctly is critical in choosing the path you want your motorcycle to follow. You must discipline yourself to look where you want to go. Look to the escape route. Look to the clear path. You're training yourself to look away from two objects that can hurt you and refocus your sight on a safe way through. Sounds simple reading it in a book, but at 50 mph it's a challenging mind game.

Proper use of the eyes is vital to a motorcyclist in terms of safety and survival. And how you interpret what your eyes are telling you makes the difference between an experienced rider and a fresh-faced rookie. Use your eyes correctly and you'll be safer, smoother and faster.

CONCENTRATION AND DISCIPLINE

Sometimes during a roadrace, a rider will fall in front of you. It's happened to me several times, but the most dramatic example was at Mid-Ohio at an AMA 250GP race. I had been chasing Jon Cornwell and finally caught him about two laps from the end of the race. We were fighting for second place. As we wheelied over the hill just before the hard right that dumped us into Thunder Alley, I got as close as I dared without actually becoming his passenger. Jon ran into the next right pretty hot, and he overdid his braking, bottomed his front fork while he leaned over and locked the front tire.

In a split second Cornwell was on his right side, crashed out of the race. I remember fighting to keep my eyes on the racetrack, on my chosen line, a job as strenuous to me at that moment as bench-pressing 300 pounds. I had been looking ahead of Cornwell's bike when he crashed, and despite the distraction of a TZ250 and rider sliding off the track in a haze of aluminum dust and debris, I kept my eyes and mind on my

In the early and mid '90s, I would spend the week riding street bikes and the weekend racing my TZ250. During the first few laps of practice, my eyes tended to be low and late to shift focus because my street-based visual habits weren't ready for the pace of a 250GP bike. The faster you ride, the quicker your eyes must move. (Brian J. Nelson)

line. As a result, my bike stayed at the desired lean angle, I made the corner and climbed onto the podium.

Using your eyes comes down to one thing: mental discipline.

A real-world street example illustrates the proper visual techniques when riding in a group. Many of us find ourselves focusing on the bike directly ahead of us, its tires or perhaps the rider's helmet. Wrong. When riding through corners in close quarters, look ahead of the bike you're following to avoid surprises like debris or traffic. If you're following closely, shift your focus ahead of the bike you're following and use your peripheral vision to maintain the proper following distance. I recommend backing off until you are comfortably behind your friend, but that isn't always realistic. You still may not be looking far enough ahead to avoid obstacles.

LOOK UP THE ROAD

The first time I met Eddie Lawson was at Laguna Seca Raceway back in 1986. We'd asked Eddie to come and coach us for a *Motorcyclist* story, and we spent the day circling Laguna ahead of and behind Eddie—mostly behind. At that

Above: Imagine being introduced to Laguna Seca by Eddie Lawson. Working on this 1986 *Motorcyclist* magazine story showed me a Grand Prix champion's world, where missing an apex by just six inches is a big mistake. (Dexter Ford, courtesy of *Motorcyclist*)

Below right: Street riders get in trouble when their bikes go fast but their eyes don't keep up. Take a lesson from Formula Extreme racer Damon Buckmaster, shown here looking at the spot his Graves Yamaha R1 race bike is about to catapult toward. Fast bike, quick eyes. (Brian J. Nelson)

time he had won two national Superbike championships and two world 500GP championships, and one of the main points he kept emphasizing was "look up the road."

"Most riders focus just ahead of their front wheel," Eddie said, "and that gives an incredible sense of speed because the ground's rushing past really fast. If you get your eyes up and look farther up the road, everything slows down, and you don't feel as overwhelmed by the speed." The best illustration of this is to imagine riding alongside a white picket fence. Look directly over at the fence and it races by in a blur of white, but look farther ahead and you can pick out individual pickets. You're still moving at the same speed, but you've simply refocused your gaze farther ahead. From this you learn a simple equation: Distance equals time.

By looking up the road or through the corner, you'll reduce your perceived speed and give yourself more time to make the proper decisions and control inputs. It's a racer's technique and will make a huge difference in your sport riding.

"Riders who don't look up the road enough will always be late on the throttle," Eddie went on, "because by the time they realize it's okay to accelerate, they've been out of the corner for quite

a while." Of course, picking up the throttle early in the corner is important to a racer, but it's an important technique for street riders as well. If your focus is too close to your front tire, you can lose your place on the road or in the corner, and everything you do will be poorly timed and awkward.

KEEP YOUR EYES MOVING

So you want to get your eyes up and look farther up the road, but how far? After all, you can't simply focus on the horizon, because there are plenty of nasty things like bumps, diesel fuel, sand and spare tires waiting to trip you. Street riders can't count on a perfect surface like roadracers can, so you need to scan the pavement, not just jump your eyes to the horizon. Scan constantly, moving your eyes from the path immediately in front of you to the farthest point you can see in the corner; as the corner unwinds in front of you, continue to scan to the farthest point. Never look so far up the road that you miss potentially dangerous obstacles in your path. The California Highway Patrol teaches the same basic technique, which it describes as "maintaining a high horizon". In other words, keep your eyes up and look far up the freeway so you can identify problems long before you reach them.

Mastering this technique requires shifting your eyes from a particular section of road or even a section of a corner. For instance, as you approach a corner, you will be looking at a spot at the corner entrance, probably where you think it's a good place to turn. Leave your eyes on that spot too long, however, and the rest of the corner will either surprise you or rush you. Move your eyes off that entrance point and

up into the corner, looking for your apex point, or the point at which you come closest to the edge of your lane. As you approach that spot, rip your eyes up again to the exit. Move them. Jump them off anything that threatens to grab your attention, like a crack in the pavement or a rock in the road.

PERIPHERAL POWER

Peripheral vision—the amount of vision you have away from your focal point—is one of the most vital attributes needed by every rider, from racer to commuter to Sunday sport bike rider. Think of peripheral vision as an awareness, one that can be enlarged and strengthened. What we're talking about is seeing without fixating, viewing without staring, gathering information that you may have previously overlooked.

EYE DRILL: VISION REVISION

Try these drills to test your peripheral vision awareness, and continue them to strengthen it.

1. Walk down the sidewalk and while staring straight ahead, count the cracks as they pass underfoot. This test is especially important for riders because you must monitor your current situation (counting the cracks) at the same time as you are looking ahead.

2. Stare into a crowd and, while maintaining a single focal point, try to pick up all movement with your peripheral vision. Developing this ability will help you move through traffic with your eyes looking ahead while maintaining enough peripheral strength to detect movement anywhere in your field of view.

3. When watching TV, look at the corner of the screen and attempt to watch the show with your peripheral vision. Use the same technique when following another rider. Look ahead of the leading rider's bike (when following relatively closely), yet maintain the leader's position in your peripheral vision. What you want to avoid is staring at the leading rider or bike.

4. Close this book momentarily, then pop it open to any page and close it again immediately. How much did you

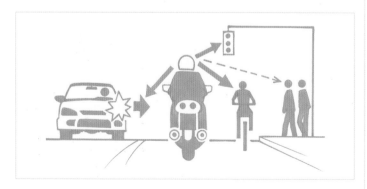

Above: The brain's primary information source is the eyes, yet many motorcyclists fail to move their eyes enough, especially as speed or weariness increase. Don't think that you have to move your head to change your focus, just move those eyes. (Brian Blades)
Below left: This rider's number-one threat is the oncoming car waiting to turn left, but he also must pay attention to the bicyclist, pedestrians and the traffic light. The main focus must be on the car, but the rider's peripheral vision must assess the remaining problems. When you learn to be much more aware of things in your peripheral vision, your street riding will become more comfortable. (Hector Cademartori)

Right: As this Moto Guzzi rider prepares to exit this downhill hairpin, his eyes are looking ahead to the exit because he has already seen the middle of the corner as he entered. Scan ahead of the bike and keep those eyes constantly moving.

read? How much of a photo did you see? Keep trying it, and work on expanding that quick bite of information. This becomes important while scanning traffic, glancing in your mirror or checking over your shoulder. Use your peripheral vision to soak in as much information as possible, in as short a time as possible. Sure, you can see a lot with a slow look over your shoulder, but commuters don't have that luxury in heavy traffic, right? Try to capture the scene the instant you view it. This becomes especially helpful for those quick glances in the mirror prior to a lane change in heavy traffic.

Work on the four drills above to enlarge your peripheral awareness. It's your awareness of objects out of your direct line of focus that is most important, so enlarging that awareness adds significantly to your riding skills. We'll discuss additional urban riding skills in chapter 9, but you can be sure many of them will deal with how you use your eyeballs.

LOOK AHEAD. RUSSELL DOES.

We've all seen shots of five-time Daytona 200 winner Scott Russell leaned over in one of Daytona's two horseshoes with his head turned toward the exit of the corner at an almost unnatural angle. There are several reasons Russell is focused on the corner exit, all of them good. Let's use Scott Russell to learn a few things about looking up the road.

STREET LESSON #2

The only way to fine-tune the way you operate your bike's controls is to give yourself more time. That means scanning farther ahead, extending your vision up the road to see corners, bumps and stop signs. If you don't get your eyes up, you'll be continually late and hurried with the controls of your bike and continually surprised by events you should have seen early and planned for accordingly. Riding smoothly is an excellent goal for street riders, and smoothness begins when the eyes look up for the big picture. The next time something surprises or shocks you, I bet your eyes will be at fault.

Above: Five-time Daytona 200 winner Scott Russell covers a lot of Daytona International Speedway in a very short time, but he "slows down the track" by getting his eyes up and looking far ahead. Anytime a rider is freaked out by speed, their eyes are usually low and looking just ahead of the front tire. Raise your horizon to feed more information to your brain. (John Flory)
Below: Despite the distraction of highly competitive traffic, Kurtis Roberts and the AMA racers keep their eyes up and moving, and their minds on the future. (Brian J. Nelson)

RUSSELL REASON #3

As Russell approaches his braking marker at the entrance to the corner, he moves his eyes off the braking area and into the apex of the corner. As the bike turns into the corner, Russell moves his eyes off the apex and to the exit of the corner, and continues to move his eyes up the track to the next braking marker he'll be using. It's an active, involved habit that requires a racer to keep the eyes moving ahead of the bike.

RUSSELL REASON #1

Remember the picket fence? Russell does, and he is looking up the racetrack to slow the information coming to him. Distance makes the difference, and Russell slows the rapidity of the information coming to him by moving his eyes up the track as far as is comfortable.

STREET LESSON #1

Street riders must modify Russell's far-reaching visual approach because you aren't guaranteed the clear, clean, gravel-free pavement of Daytona. Street riders must learn to constantly scan back and forth from the bike's front tire to the farthest point you can comfortably see rather than just swivel your eyes to the horizon.

STREET LESSON #3

A racer's eye-movement pattern makes sense for street riders as well. If you leave your eyes on the corner entrance too long, you might miss the radius of the corner or some dangerous debris in the corner. Be sure to keep your eyes moving, get them off the entrance to the middle of the corner and, as you approach the middle, look to the exit. Make the eyes' movements smooth and controlled. The faster you ride, the farther you'll need to look ahead of your bike.

RUSSELL REASON #2

By looking up the racetrack, Russell can plan and time his control inputs better. The amazing thing is what happens with the throttle. As you'll learn in chapter 5, early application of the throttle is a good thing, and the only way Russell's brain knows to begin opening the throttle is that his eyes are looking at the corner exit, even before he's at the corner's apex. (We'll define *apex* as the point at which the rider is closest to the inside edge of the lane or track.)

Tune-up Time

When did you last visit the optometrist? If you're like most Americans, you have your eyes checked only when you break your glasses, lose your contacts or fail the driver's license eye exam. There you are, possibly riding with faulty equipment, a set of eyes that aren't truly seeing everything they can. As a motorcyclist, your life depends on your vision, so an annual eye exam might be one of the best steps you can take to extend your riding career.

Many riders wear glasses or contacts while riding. Glasses can be a hassle to fit inside the helmet and are an obvious danger during a crash because of their proximity to the eyes. They present another surface for dirt and debris to settle upon, and another layer to fog during cold or wet weather.

Contacts wearers have found varying degrees of success, mostly depending on how much wind enters their helmets. One of the most famous contacts-wearing roadracers is Freddie Spencer. He was often photographed with tape surrounding his face shield for an extra layer to protect against wind entering his Arai. He wasn't always able to keep his lenses in place successfully, but that difficulty came during the stress of a 500cc Grand Prix, when it's probably difficult to remember to blink. Street riders should find it easier.

One truly miraculous solution for riders forced to wear corrective lenses has been laser surgery that corrects nearsightedness and astigmatisms. I underwent this surgery at the beginning of 1995 after racing for six years with glasses, and the results continue to be terrific. Two things pushed me toward laser surgery. The first was a very rainy 1994 season, which had me frequently cursing my foggy, wet glasses. Second, my glasses left me with a cut on my cheek after I crashed a test bike in Germany. The gash could have been my eye, so after a few months of research, I got lasered.

This book isn't a source for laser surgery information, but this surgery is a tremendous solution for nearsighted motorcycle riders. You depend heavily on your eyes, wear constraining headgear and ride in a windy, dirty, sometimes wet environment. I encourage you to look into it. Who knows what perfect vision can do for you?

Again, a street rider must scan the asphalt to check for debris and bumps, while a racer can be more certain of pavement consistency.

SELF-ANALYSIS

Since the eyes are so critical to our sport, it's important to recognize the problems that stem from improper visual habits. Failing to master this single skill can cause a wide variety of riding problems. Among them are the following:

1. Running wide in a corner. If you had slow-motion video of a rider going wide in a corner, you'd probably notice that her eyes quit looking through the corner. Instead, her eyes either got caught on something like a pothole or rock, or failed to scan through the corner as the bike entered it. Once again, keep your eyes moving ahead of the bike.

2. Hitting stationary objects. Target fixation is a simple term, but it brings an ugly result. A rider's eyes get caught on something like a pothole, car fender, curbing—and the bike follows the gaze. Tearing your eyes off something that draws your interest is like ripping Velcro apart—but it's a skill worth mastering.

3. Being late on the throttle. Applying the throttle (lightly) as early as possible after turning into a corner is a critical aspect of riding well. We will talk all about it in chapter 5, but the reason many riders are late on the throttle is their eyes: They're simply not looking up the road far enough. No matter how many times you've ridden through a corner, your brain needs your eyes to reaffirm that the pavement does indeed still exist and that your right wrist can begin to gently roll on the throttle.

4. Being overwhelmed and surprised. Riders continuously overwhelmed with speed are simply focusing too close to their front tire. Distance slows things down and gives the brain more time to deal with everything from an encroaching car to an upcoming corner.

5. Entering a corner far too slowly. While braking for a corner, it's easy to leave your eyes on whatever you were using to gauge your speed and braking distance, and your entrance speed suffers. You stay on the brakes too long because you need your eyes to look into the corner to correctly gauge the corner's radius, pavement, etc. Isn't it interesting to find that one of the main secrets to good entrance speed is the eyes?

LESSONS FROM THE RACETRACK

CLEAN IS CLEAR The top professional racers visit their helmet representative between every practice for either a face-shield cleaning or a completely new face shield. The tuners take plenty of time making sure the bike's windscreen is clean and smudge free. Everyone involved knows the importance of giving the eyes the clearest view possible.

LOOK AHEAD OF THE COMPETITION Beginning racers soon discover that if they stare at the rider they just caught, their speed will match that rider's speed exactly. Racers learn to look ahead of the rider they hope to pass, monitoring that rider's place on the track with quick glances and use of peripheral vision.

GET LASERED Getting rid of your glasses or contacts really helps, especially in dusty venues or the rain. Laser surgery eliminates the need for glasses and seems tailor-made for racers.

CHAPTER 4

STEER THAT THING

LET'S MOVE BEYOND COUNTERSTEERING AND TRULY CONTROL THE MOTORCYCLE

Ask 10 riders how to steer a motorcycle and you get 10 different responses. For the hard-to-find answer to this simple but important question, we sent a rider down his favorite road for three experimental passes. On the first pass, he took his hands off the handlebar and tried to steer the bike by pushing his knees against the tank, leaning his weight to the inside of the turn and pushing on the foot pegs with his feet. Our rider scared himself silly before grabbing the bar halfway through the first corner because the bike wasn't responding quickly enough to match the road's direction. On the next pass, he took his feet off the foot pegs and steered by pushing and pulling on the handgrips but not twisting the throttle or squeezing the brakes. He found it better than the first approach, but still not quite right. On the final run, he left his feet on the pegs and again pushed and pulled on the handlebar to change the bike's direction, using the throttle and brakes. The third pass made it obvious that we control and steer a road-going motorcycle at the handlebar, but the body and control action have some significant effects as well. As you'll discover in this chapter, there are four ways to steer your motorcycle, but only after you master the primary one—countersteering—can you truly experiment with the other three, expert-level methods.

It isn't important that you understand the physics involved in countersteering (basically, it works because as the handlebar is pushed, the front tire deflects, and the bike leans into the corner). It is important, however, that you understand how pushing and pulling on your handgrips affects your motorcycle, and how the understanding and application of this technique can give you an unbelievably high degree of bike control. In fact, you can forget the term *countersteering*. Just remember this: How and when you apply pressure to the handlebar helps you do everything from dodging potholes to winning world championships. The other three techniques of steering that are discussed in this chapter can be described as finesse moves, and as your riding improves, you'll learn that this sport is all about finesse. So your first task is to understand how to effectively countersteer.

Left: Chapter 2 covered the basics of motorcycle control, but this chapter will reveal the vital inputs necessary to place the motorcycle exactly where you want it, regardless of whether you're on the street or the track. (Dennis Morrison)

Right: As an experiment, we asked our third rider in line to enter this corner with his hands off the bars. The bike began to lean, but it never steered toward the apex, and he was forced to grab the bars to avoid running straight. This is a graphic way to emphasize that steering techniques revolve around the rider's ability to use at least one hand on the bar, preferably the hand that brakes and accelerates. (Brian Blades)

Above: Caught here teaching at the Freddie Spencer School, I'm pointing out the correct line to a following student, but also illustrating how light a touch we can have on the handlebar and still turn effectively. In this case, my left hand is completely off the bar, so it provides no input at all. (Dennis Morrison)
Below: Wide handlebars provide tremendous leverage for those who countersteer aggressively, allowing this bike to be turned quickly with little steering effort. Ride relaxed on a wide-barred bike or unintended steering inputs will create a wobble at speed. In fact, any bike will wobble if the rider has rigid arms and a death grip on the bars. (Brian Blades)

PUSH AND PULL

As the bike's speed increases, the gyroscopic effect of its spinning wheels (and brake discs, chain, transmission, etc.) creates ever-increasing stability. So a bike traveling at 80 mph requires more muscle at the handlebar to steer than it would at 30 mph. Lazily steering a bike into a turn requires so little effort that few riders recognize the physical process involved, and that's why you'll get so many different answers to the question of steering. A rider might actually think she is turning by "leaning" into the corner, but unfortunately she won't be able to turn her bike much faster until she becomes more aware of the pressure at the handgrips.

As you experiment with countersteering, you'll notice the bike changes direction in relation to the amount of force you apply at the bars. Push lightly on the inside bar, and the bike lazes into the corner. Punch at the inside bar, and the bike snaps over a bit too uncontrollably. Push on the inside bar and pull on the outside bar, and the effect is sensational; the combined push and pull serve to put the bike into a lean angle almost effortlessly.

Notice how much effort you need to turn the bike at higher speeds. Practice pushing and pulling on the handlebar to help overcome the gyroscopic effects of the wheels. As your experimentation continues, you'll never again cross over the centerline to help straighten a curvy section of road, because you'll want to

enjoy snapping the bike back and forth through the bends. I feel sorry for riders who stray from their lane to straighten a road—they're not only demonstrating their lack of motorcycle control, they're also missing out on all the fun.

ROW, DON'T PUNCH

Smooth, relaxed hands are a key ingredient for good riding inputs. With that in mind, don't overpower the handlebar during direction changes. Don't punch or lunge at the grips, but push and pull them in a smooth, controlled motion. You can certainly turn a fast-moving bike aggressively, but too much aggression will have the chassis out of shape as the fork and shock springs rebound after the bike is "thrown" into the corner. Anytime you're waiting for your chassis to settle down, you're basically out of control. Back off the muscular handlebar inputs and your smoothness will pay off in better chassis manners, improved tire wear and reduced heart rate.

FORCE AT THE HANDGRIPS

Because the handgrips are the main steering points, it makes sense to reduce the amount of extra weight, or force, being carried by the bars. Using your stomach, back and chest muscles to hold yourself in place will greatly reduce the amount of weight borne by the handlebar, allowing you to further refine the force used for steering the bike. It becomes abundantly clear why professional roadracers work out so frequently, and why torso strength is a main focus of their efforts.

Imagine welding a steel bar from your handlebar to your bike's frame. Every movement of your front tire would be immediately transferred into the chassis, creating a wobble, weave—or worse. This is exactly what happens when you grip the bars too tightly before, during or after steering

Above: Relax. Let your elbows hang naturally, not tucked in or flying out aggressively. Keep your eyes level with the horizon, not tilted with the bike. Relax your spine, because as soon as you sit bolt upright, your elbows will lock and you'll lose front-end feel. (Brian Blades)

Below right: In terms of using the throttle, most turns have three parts. At the entrance, the throttle is closed because the brakes are probably being applied to set the bike's speed. The throttle stays shut (white squares) until the bike has turned into the corner, at which point the throttle is opened very slightly, to neutral or maintenance throttle (black dashes). Maintenance throttle lasts until the exit is visible and the bike can begin standing up off the apex, meaning it might last 10 feet or 80 feet, depending on the corner. As the exit becomes visible and the lane is clear, accelerating throttle will help stand the bike up (solid black line). The more lean angle you use, the slower these throttle movements must be. (Hector Cademartori)

inputs. Every movement of the front end moves those clenched arms and consequently disrupts the bike's stability. While it takes some muscle to push and pull on the handlebar, you must keep a relaxed grip and fight the urge to strangle the handgrips. Learn to make a direction change and then relax to let the bike remain settled and stable rather than induce problems with a too-tight grip. This further emphasizes the importance of torso strength, because it's the stomach and back muscles that allow you to take your weight off your arms, and off the handgrips.

Consciously remind yourself to relax. Not only will your bike feel more planted on the road, you'll gain more traction information from the tires, allowing you to improve everything from cornering speed to lean angle. If you continue to hang on too tightly, you'll never read what your bike is trying to tell you, and any riding improvement will be much tougher to realize. And if you never relax at the handlebar, you will never experience the additional three ways to steer your bike.

ADDITIONAL STEERING SECRETS

Pushing and pulling on the handlebar, or countersteering, gets the job done, but there's a whole lot more to the steering story. In fact, the four ways of steering a bike don't stand alone. You don't simply pick one and then apply that one skill to the next corner you approach. That would be similar to a golfer focusing on a slow back swing while disregarding weight shift, keeping his head down, and ignoring all the other skills needed to properly hit the ball. Sure, mastering one skill will certainly help, but the careful mixing of all the skills involved in a consistently great golf swing is what it takes to get on the world tour. Similarly, motorcyclists can see that while an understanding of countersteering helps you to ride better, to really ride well you need to apply a few more skills.

COUNTERSTEERING ASSISTANT #1:
THROTTLE STEERING

We're going to talk more about throttle steering in chapter 5, but I want to touch on the fundamentals here. A motorcycle's throttle controls speed, but what you're focusing on here is the throttle's effect on lean angle. Remember when we talked about steering and then relaxing at the handlebar? Using the throttle to modulate lean angle will allow you to relax your grip on the bars, which in turn will allow you to feel more of what the front tire is trying to tell you about traction. The end result is an increase in your speed, safety and confidence as you ride. Since the throttle can modulate your lean angle, the need to push and pull at the handlebar is reduced.

Your bike will fall into a corner when the throttle is closed (off-throttle), it will stand up out of the corner when the throttle is rolled open (on-throttle) and will hold a constant lean angle when the throttle is slightly cracked open (maintenance throttle).

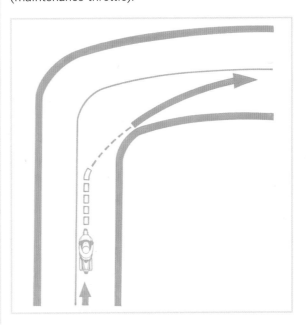

I include the terms in parenthesis to establish a vocabulary to better discuss throttle steering. *On-throttle* means accelerating throttle; the bike is actually gaining speed. In contrast, *maintenance throttle* is the most minor application of throttle imaginable, twisting the right grip so slightly that the carburetor slides or fuel-injection butterflies barely move. In fact, the motorcycle's speed might actually be decreasing with maintenance throttle. There's a huge difference between maintenance throttle and accelerating throttle. The difference between on-throttle and maintenance throttle also has a great deal to do with who wins world championships and who high-sides themselves into oblivion. So let's talk more about the throttle's effect on steering.

You enter the corner *off-throttle* and initiate the turn. The bike banks into the corner and continues to fall because the throttle is closed. As you reach the lean angle necessary to make the apex of the corner at the speed you've chosen, you can push on the outside bar to arrest the increasing lean angle. Or you can crack open the throttle to maintenance to achieve the same effect. Going to maintenance throttle at this point will be a much smoother way of arresting the lean angle, and as the corner opens

One of the highlights of my 18 months as the editor of MotoGP.com was riding Kenny Roberts, Jr.'s championship-winning Suzuki RGv500. I rode the missile on the Monday following the final GP of 2000 at Phillip Island, and imagine my surprise when Valentino Rossi zapped past on the right kink before Lukey Heights. Look how well Valentino has pointed his bike down to the apex in preparation for the exit. I'm a few inches wide, which illustrates the potential problem of too much initial throttle. Both of us have picked up the throttle to arrest the lean angle and get the bikes to the apex, but I lack the feel needed on a bike making 190 horsepower. (Gold & Goose)

Rear Brake Drag

There is an alternative to closing the throttle to tighten your cornering line, and that's dragging the rear brake. This racetrack technique is especially easy in left-hand corners due to the placement of the brake pedal, and is the reason why thumb-operated rear brakes have been appearing on race bikes over the past few years. The problem with closing the throttle mid-corner on the racetrack is that you're often much nearer the traction limit than you would be on the street, and closing the throttle transfers weight onto the front tire, a front tire that might not be able to handle it. Instead, racers have learned to leave the throttle steady and drag a bit of rear brake. That said, let's be clear that using the brakes and throttle at the same time is a track skill that simply isn't a part of street riding. If you want to pick up the throttle, you should first be off the brakes, and if you want to squeeze the brakes, you should first close the throttle. But a little dab of the rear brake will help steer the bike into the corner.

up, you can simply roll the throttle on to help the bike stand up out of the corner.

A *closed throttle* moves a motorcycle's weight forward onto the front tire. As that happens, the fork compresses and the bike's steering geometry tightens, encouraging the bike to steer. As the throttle is snuck open to maintenance throttle, the weight moves rearward, coming off the front tire and allowing the fork to extend slightly. As the throttle is then rolled open to on-throttle, the fork extends completely as the bike's weight is borne mostly by the rear tire. The extended fork helps widen the bike's cornering radius and

helps stand the bike up off the corner.

Focus your skill on the fine touch needed to sneak open the throttle after the turn-in. Applying maintenance throttle to arrest the lean angle is a huge reason why some riders continue to miss apexes and overshoot corners, running wide at the exits. These riders get greedy and open the throttle too early while entering the corner, or they open the throttle too hard, skipping maintenance throttle as they jump right to on-throttle. Either mistake prevents the bike from turning down to the apex, but both are also easy to correct: Leave the throttle shut longer! Don't go to the throttle until the bike has been turned into the corner, and then go to it very gently so the bike continues to carve the radius you've selected to reach the apex. So when can you open the throttle? As soon as possible after the bike has been turned into the corner. But the earlier you open it, the more smoothly you must open it.

Smoothness is even more important if you have a powerful bike, because a small turn of the right handgrip means a lot of horsepower, especially at high rpm. This lesson really hit home when I guest-rode Kenny Roberts, Jr.'s, world championship–winning Suzuki 500. Because of the instant power, I found myself leaving the throttle closed longer than I expected simply because once the bike began carbureting, it wanted to stand up and lunge off the corner. Roberts and his ilk use the throttle to steer, and my laps aboard his bike brought home how smoothly the right hand must move on high-horsepower machines.

COUNTERSTEERING ASSISTANT #2: LEG PRESSURE

One of the biggest drawbacks to pushing and pulling on the handlebar to turn a motorcycle is the unintended inputs you make when you either squeeze the grips too tightly or lean your weight onto the handlebar. One great way to lighten the handlebar's load is to utilize your outside leg to help steer the bike into the corner. By placing the inside of your knee and thigh against the tank, you can apply pressure to help initiate tipping the bike into a corner.

The truth about this technique is not that you're steering with your knees, but that you're focusing your steering efforts on your legs, not your hands. You are still inputting pressure to the handlebar as you push on the fuel tank with your leg, but because you're focused on your leg movement, your hands are relaxed, and the weight on the handlebar is minimal. The more relaxed you are at the handlebar, the better the ride will be, and this leg pressure technique is exactly what many of us need to loosen a too-tight grip.

To prove that leg pressure alone doesn't steer a motorcycle very efficiently, try moving your hands from the handlebar to the fairing edges, fuel tank or your lap. With your hands off the grips, your anchor is gone and you have

Help from the Front Brake

To take throttle steering a step further, think about touching the front brake lever to help steer the bike into the corner. If closed throttle puts weight forward and compresses the fork, a small touch on the front brake will carry this technique a bit further, allowing the bike to turn into the corner in less time and distance, and with less handlebar pressure.

You might be thinking that if you touch the brake lever to help your bike steer into the corner, your bike will stand up. Yes, it will—if your touch is too harsh, too grabby, too abrupt. Ease that brake lever on. Slow those fingers down. We'll discuss this technique more in chapter 6 as we study the art and science of trail-braking, and why you need to master trail-braking to stay alive on the street and win at the track.

Top: Street riders must get in the habit of leaving their finger(s) on the front brake lever after they've completed their braking so any unexpected debris in a blind corner can be dealt with in less time and distance. Remember that the most important thing is not always how long it takes to stop your bike, but how far your bike has traveled before you get on the brakes.
Above: Don't just read about it, do it! Steer your bike into a corner with leg pressure against the fuel tank and feel your torso tighten. In this case, it's left leg against the tank to tilt the Aprilia into a right-hand corner. Note that the left hand is off the bar to emphasize the role the leg plays in steering. (Brian Blades)

nothing to brace yourself with as your leg pushes on the tank—and the bike doesn't turn. Your hand on the handlebar counteracts the push of the knee, and that's enough force at the handgrip to turn the motorcycle.

While you're sitting there reading this book, lift your right leg up and over toward your left. Do it again, and feel what happens to your stomach and back muscles. Feel them tighten to support and balance you? When that happens at the entrance of a corner, your hands are left unloaded and can better use the brakes, downshift and feel for front tire traction information. As the leg moves, the torso tightens and the arms relax.

The leg pressure technique can help the initial turn-in at the entrance of the corner. As you discovered when you rode down your favorite road without your feet on the pegs, the legs can help smooth direction changes and damp or modulate overaggressive steering inputs. Also, the outside leg can help modulate lean angle at mid-corner, often more smoothly than a push on the handlebar, so you can continue to smooth your riding. Of course, riding smoothness is something you'll seek all your life, and using the outside leg is a technique that utilizes pressure at the handlebar yet diverts your attention to the outside leg.

Left: Using your outside knee against the fuel tank will tighten your stomach and back muscles, allowing you to relax your arms. This technique helps steer the bike, but more important, it reminds you that relaxed arms and hands are vital. Note: All riding apparel shown is included not because of sponsorship, but because it works very well in the real world. (Hence all the bugs and grime on my Aerostich suit!) (Brian Blades)

Right: As an "on-board engineer," your ability to move your body makes a huge difference in how your bike works. Placing your weight low and to the inside of the corner helps load the inside foot peg and will allow you to run less lean angle at the same speed. Let's look at a left-hand corner and three different body positions.

A. This rider is doing everything possible to work against the bike by sitting up on the high side and riding with a straight inside arm. This "style" requires more lean angle at a given speed, or requires less speed to maintain the same lean angle. Hmmm...slower and less safe, not a good approach. This rider will drag parts (foot pegs, sidestand and his own toes) on the ground very early and will crash frequently, without knowing why.
B. This racer is taking full advantage of his ability to move off the bike, loading the inside foot peg, using his outside leg to grip the tank and tightening his stomach and back muscles to hold himself in place. Perfect...for the track. On the street, that extended knee and dipped head will set off big alarms in police cars, but the main problem is the speed this style encourages. By the time you're hanging off and tucking in on the street, you're well into the 30-percent safety margin we all need for the inevitable surprises. That said, your ability to get into this position is important because hanging off drastically allows the bike to run less lean angle through unexpected gravel or water. Practice this style, but not the speed that can go with it.
C. This rider has moved his butt slightly to the inside of the bike to load the foot peg and is leading with his chin, helping to get the arms bent. The outside knee helps steer the bike, and the inside knee stays in to avoid that illegal look cops hate. This is a perfect street-riding position because it works with the bike while reminding the rider that Highway 2 isn't a racetrack. (Brian Blades)

COUNTERSTEERING ASSISTANT #3: WEIGHTING YOUR FOOTPEGS

If your motorcycle weighs 450 pounds and you weigh 150 pounds, it's obvious that your body weight is a significant portion of the total mass rolling down the road—in this case, 25 percent. What you do with your body has a dramatic effect on how and when the bike steers, so shifting rider weight is the third assisting technique we'll discuss with regard to steering.

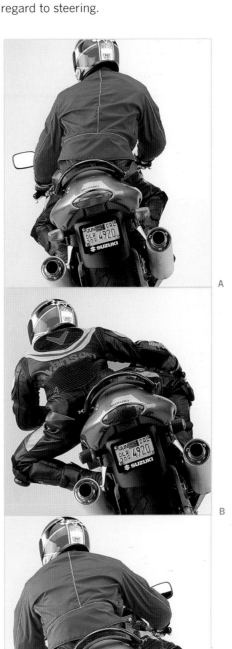

A

B

C

Above and right: Many of us arrive on the street-bike scene from the dirt, and there are some significant differences in body position during cornering. Dirt riders put the bike down beneath them, inside foot off the peg, butts balanced on the outside edge of the seat, weight on the outside foot peg. Street riders put their weight on the inside foot peg, chin and chest to the inside, butts to the inside edge of the seat. When a rider moves his body around the bike, he affects everything from steering quickness to lean angle to stability. On the racetrack, this position can be taken to extremes. (Jeff Allen)

We've all ridden a bicycle or motorcycle without our hands on the handlebar and discovered that we can still turn corners. Or we can, at least, lean into them. The direction change isn't sudden or even firm, but the bike can be guided, however vaguely, by a shift in the rider's weight.

If you coast down the road with your hands off the handlebar, which way do you lean to initiate a turn to the right? You lean to the right, or into the corner. You start moving your shoulders when you want your coasting bike to begin the turn, and that's the exact habit you want to continue when you place your hands back onto the handlebar. Because the weight of your torso and head is relatively high in comparison to the motorcycle's center of mass (which is close to the bike's crankshaft), the movement of the head and shoulders has a significant impact on the handling of the motorcycle. Discover it for yourself: Stand up and then lean your head and shoulders to the right. Feel the weight come onto your right foot? That will load the bike's right foot peg, helping the bike steer right.

To be sure you're loading that inside foot peg, get in the habit of leading the bike into the corner with your chin and, to a lesser extent, the center zipper of your jacket. Be sure the zipper is either centered over the middle of the fuel tank or slightly to the inside, toward the direction you are turning. What you're trying to accomplish is simple: You want to use your weight to help the bike turn, and as you know from

your hands-free experiment, the bike begins turning when you move your body weight toward the inside of the corner, onto the inside foot peg.

Longtime dirt bike riders have trouble with this skill because they're used to sitting up on top of the bike and putting the machine down beneath them in the corner. Leaving your weight way up high like that upsets a street bike, masks traction feedback, overworks the suspension, uses up valuable ground clearance and just doesn't make sense. On the pavement, use your weight to help the bike fall into the corner by placing your torso toward the inside of the corner.

But there's more to it. The timing of this weight change is critical, as is the placement of your weight onto the inside foot peg. Move your body weight too early, and the bike will fade into the corner before you're ready to commit. Move your body weight too late, and the bike will resist the steering input—and when it finally comes, it may upset things while you're leaned over. The difficulty in mastering the body position steering skills lies in the timing of the weight shift onto the inside foot peg.

For a strong sense of how well weighting a foot peg works, cruise down the road and stand up on your pegs. While standing, lift a foot off the peg and notice the bike turn immediately the other way, in the direction of the weighted peg.

Through a set of esses, the timing of your body movements can significantly reduce the steering pressure needed at the handlebar. Think about it. You've got a quarter of the total rolling mass moving around on top of the bike. How and when that mass is moved becomes critical to smoothness, and to winning races.

As you begin to experiment with the movement (and the timing of that movement), focus on how you're moving your body. Begin by dipping your head and shoulders into the corner, but start to slide your butt toward the inside of the corner too. Keep your knees in—save the radical knee out, hanging off, for the racetrack. Take advantage of an inch or two of butt movement to help the bike steer. Be careful not to tug on the handlebar during your weight shifts. Remember, the handlebar makes all significant direction changes, so any input will either alter your course or cause instability. Instead, use your thighs to help move your weight across the seat, with the balls of your feet on the foot pegs. Don't stand up as you move, but use your legs to raise up just enough so that your butt slides easily across the seat. You'll find the task much more difficult if

you have your heels or arches on the pegs, so concentrate on getting either your toes or the balls of your feet to carry your weight. Riding with your toes or the balls of your feet on the foot pegs provides a more dynamic feel on the bike.

Finally, a reminder: Don't confuse body movement with foot peg weighting. You should be able to move your body all over your bike as you cruise down the road in a straight line with both pegs equally weighted, but as soon as you weight a foot peg, the bike will turn.

STEERING PRACTICE MAKES PERFECT

You practice your steering every time you ride a bike, but a bit of focused practice will go a long way toward the goal of bike control. Find yourself a clean parking lot or deserted road and focus on steering.

1. The first experiment is to simply push on one of the handgrips at any speed above a walk. Push it slowly. Push it quickly. Push easy. Push hard. Notice how much more effort it takes to steer a bike at 60 mph than at 30 mph.

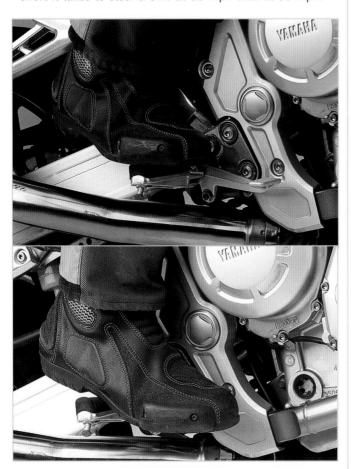

Place the balls of your feet on the foot pegs to better weight the pegs during direction changes. Riders who place their mid-foot or heel on the pegs will feel sluggish when moving their weight around the bike, and if the toes dangle down, it's easy to catch them on the pavement while leaned over. When using the rear brake or shifter, use your toes to move the lever, rocking the foot on the foot peg for maximum feel. Don't take your foot off the peg to shift or brake because you'll be far too rough with the input. Once you make the control input, place the toes back on the foot peg. (Brian Blades)

2. Add a pull on the opposite bar. Really turns quickly, doesn't it? As if you had power steering.

3. Tighten up your stomach and chest muscles, and relax your arms as much as possible. Quit leaning on the bars and hold yourself in position with your torso. Now use the same push and pull movements, but notice that the inputs aren't polluted by the weight of your body.

4. With your torso taut, use your legs to push against the tank, steering the bike with pressure from your knee and thigh. To turn right, push your left knee and inside thigh against the fuel tank. You are still countersteering, but the leg pressure tightens your stomach to support your body and this, in turn, relaxes your arms.

5. While changing lanes, see how quickly your bike will steer from the upright, straight-ahead position. Change lanes slowly and easily. Change lanes quickly and efficiently. You'll notice that when you change lanes quickly, you must exert pressure to realign the bike in the new lane, but when you change lanes slowly, the bike realigns itself. Those gyros want to go straight.

6. Follow your buddy at a safe distance and mirror her steering inputs while riding down a deserted road. If your buddy flicks the bike right, you flick it right. If she fades left and then snaps the bike upright, do the same. This is a good way to practice your strength and reaction skills.

7. Steer your bike back and forth in second gear with and without the throttle open. Notice how nicely the bike stands up from being leaned over when the throttle is open. Notice how heavy the bike feels when you steer it out of any lean angle without opening the throttle.

8. Continue to steer your bike back and forth at various speeds, and experiment with moving your chest across the gas tank and your weight onto the foot peg in the direction you want to go. Use your thigh muscles to move your butt across the seat, while your toes or the balls of your feet are on the pegs. You'll find it awkward to shift your weight unless your feet are correctly placed on the foot pegs.

COMPLICATED COURSE ALTERATIONS

Steering technique is all about smooth combinations. Push on the handlebar, push on the tank with your outside leg, lean your weight onto the inside foot peg and don't forget to use that throttle correctly. The best riders do these things almost automatically, yet they worked hard on integrating the skills. The bottom line is you must understand countersteering and how pushing and pulling on the handlebar turns the motorcycle. This must become second nature to you, ingrained and understood, just like the proper use of

This shot illustrates Anthony Gobert and company's use of their bodies to help their hard-charging Superbikes change direction, but their example helps the street rider as well. Weight the inside foot peg and lead with your helmet's chinbar to mimic the racers' technique to get their bike transitioned from left to right with minimal difficulty. (Brian J. Nelson)

LESSONS FROM THE RACETRACK

FITNESS The physical challenge of steering a fast-moving race bike stresses a rider's torso, legs, arms and neck, as well as his cardiovascular fitness. If you're looking for a reason to work out, consider this: You can bet your riding will improve as you drop fat and gain muscle. Racers focus on sit-ups and push-ups as well as plenty of legwork to allow them to move around the bike without pushing and pulling on the handlebar. Jogging, riding dirt bikes, mountain biking—anything that adds leg strength is a good way to increase strength for riding. If you have access to a gym, you can vary your workout. But don't let the lack of a gym be your excuse. Most of these activities can be done in and around your home.

BODY WEIGHT TIMING While street riders might only shift their weight slightly before entering a corner, racers tend to hang much of their bodies off the inside of the bike in an effort to use their weight to help the bike turn. Since body movement radically affects a light race bike's handling, racers must learn to time their weight shift just right. Shift your weight too early and the bike begins fading toward the corner before you are ready to make the steering input. Shift your weight too late and the bike, already committed to the corner, will bobble and wobble as you lunge to the inside. Get it right, and the body weight change perfectly matches the steering input, and the bike feels as if it is turning itself.

MORE BODY, LESS LEAN ANGLE Watch your favorite MotoGP star and observe his corner exits. The rider will stand the bike up off the apex by actually leaning farther off the inside of the bike, in essence, pushing the bike away from his body. It's a subtle move, but this technique allows the bike to maintain the radius needed to execute the turn yet remain more upright for better traction using the meat of the rear tire. Street riders can use this technique if you're surprised by a lane full of gravel when you need to make a turn. Hanging farther off the motorcycle allows the same cornering radius with less lean angle.

STEERING DAMPERS A steering damper (not dampener) controls unwanted motion of the steering head. When accelerating over a rough section of pavement, it's not uncommon for the handlebar to oscillate quickly, or head-shake. The damper prevents this flopping back and forth. Properly set up, a steering damper should have little or no effect during normal riding. You should be able to feel its drag when you force the handlebar side-to-side while at a standstill, but having it set too tight will affect straight-line stability, the same way too-tight steering-stem bearings feel. Not many street bikes need them, but most high-performance sport bikes and all race bikes do and, like suspension components, they will benefit from timely rebuilds.

your eyes. Then you begin adding the little touches, like exact throttle control, a bit of outside leg, a small weight shift. Next thing you know, people are either telling you how smoothly you ride on the street, or they're handing you trophies at the racetrack.

You can certainly see why good riders love the corners, and how a clear, concise understanding and execution of the four ways to steer a bike adds an entirely new dimension to riding a motorcycle. Suddenly you're able to put your bike within inches of your desired line rather than just herd it toward the corner. Because you can tighten and widen your cornering line at will, corners with difficult configurations become an enjoyable challenge rather than the scary mess they are now. When a pothole suddenly appears from underneath the car ahead, a quick push at the bars gets you safely around it. And when you arrive at that snaky section of road where poor riders simply cut straight through regardless of the solid yellow line, you'll find true joy in banking your bike back and forth, left and right, and wishing the corners never ended.

CHAPTER 5

ON THE GAS

MASTERING MOTORCYCLING'S MOST ABUSED CONTROL

This chapter is about coming to terms with the throttle and learning how to properly use this extremely exciting control. Sheer speed will always be a thrill, but that thrill must be balanced against the real world's unforgiving venue of tree-lined canyons, car-filled streets and prowling radar traps. And I'm willing to bet that by the time you've digested the techniques put forth in this book, outright speed will be significantly less thrilling than a perfect cornering line, precise use of brakes while downshifting and your increasing skill on that winding back road.

Throttle misuse can be blamed for the majority of single-bike accidents because a few seconds of full throttle on almost any modern motorcycle will result in triple-digit speeds. We've got 600cc sport bikes running 10-second

quarter-miles and big-bore machines threatening to run into the nines, right off the showroom floor.

Hold the throttle open a bit longer, and the 600s top out at over 150 mph, while the open-class machines blow past 180 mph, throttles pinned. This type of speed is fine out on El Mirage dry lake during a Southern California Timing Association speed meet, and you might even know a public highway where you can get away with running your bike to redline in top gear, but the majority of America's roads are no place for big speed. Too bad that throttle is so easy to twist, and its results so hard to control.

Let's face it, any idiot can accelerate hard. In fact, the idiots prove their ability every Sunday morning around the world when they add their names to the statistical charts of single-bike accidents attributed to speed. Those are the skid marks that begin just before the corner and continue straight into the guardrail or tree, or off the cliff. The real challenge is mastering the other aspects that exact throttle management brings to your riding.

Used skillfully, the twist grip is more than an accelerator, because it helps you change the bike's direction.

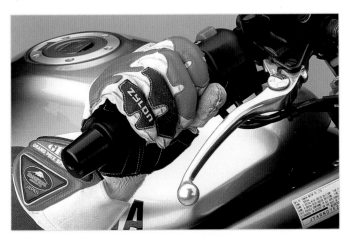

Left: Getting to this point intentionally and repeatedly speaks volumes about throttle control, a skill that expert riders work on every moment of every ride. The more horsepower your bike makes, the slower your throttle hand must move. (Brian Blades)

Above: With the performance of sport bikes these days, wide-open throttle is pretty spectacular. But like a contemporary motorcycle's powerful brakes, the throttle must be treated like a rheostat, not an on/off switch. Roll it on and off, don't stab it. (Brian Blades)

Above right: Big speed in the right environment can be safer than 40 mph downtown, so search out drag strips, roadracing tracks and other legal top-speed venues if you're hooked on mph. The El Mirage Southern California Timing Association meet is shown here. (Author's collection)

As discussed in chapter 4, the throttle is also a steering device.

You enter most corners off the throttle and on the brakes. A motorcycle turns better if the throttle is closed slightly, inducing the forward weight transfer, which aids in at least the direction change by loading the front tire and collapsing the fork. Also, a slowing motorcycle will continue to fall into the corner, so that closed throttle really helps to get a bike steered.

Opening the throttle transfers weight off the front tire and onto the rear tire, extending the fork in the process, and encourages the bike to either hold its present lean angle or straighten up, depending upon how much throttle is used (or how much horsepower your bike makes). That's why it can feel awkward to steer a bike while under hard acceleration, when the fork is at full extension and the rear suspension is squatting. Think about it: The accelerating throttle and resultant extended fork make your bike hesitant to steer simply because your bike's front-end geometry is at its most stable and least flickable (steerable). Roll off the throttle, and then the fork compresses and the bike becomes more willing to turn. You're actually adjusting your front steering geometry, taking advantage of the throttle's effect on weight transfer, to help steer the bike. Sure, you can force a bike to steer into a corner with the throttle open, but it will take longer (time and distance) to reach your desired apex. Make a habit of closing the throttle at corner entrances. This should work out perfectly, since that's also a great place to use the brakes to set your entrance speed.

BETWEEN OFF AND ON

Operate the throttle gently. Squeeze it closed. Roll it off. Feel it touch the stop. Ease it from on to off. Get the idea? I'm talking about breaking the habit of snapping the throttle off in a synapse-quick jerk of the right wrist. When you drop the throttle, the acceleration that was loading the rear wheel immediately becomes deceleration, and the weight of the motorcycle is thrown forward.

But that's not the main reason to be smooth when closing the throttle. The main reason has to do with human reactions and human hands. If you snap the throttle off, your next move will be to grab at the brake lever, which can upset the bike enough to pull your attention away from the upcoming corner, intersection or hazard.

When you grab the front brake, you might actually lengthen your stopping distance because the fork bottoms and the tire locks, either skidding or causing the bike's rear end to actually leave the ground. At that point, an understandable sense of fear makes you let go of the front brake lever, and the stopping distance is lengthened again—often with painful consequences.

So let's go right to the root of the problem and focus on closing that throttle in a smooth, controlled manner, because

Above: Steering and suspension performance are affected by how the rider moves weight forward or backward on the motorcycle. The fork compresses under braking and extends under acceleration, and you should learn to use this to help turn the bike into a corner (off-throttle) or simply ride smoothly across rough railroad tracks (on-throttle).
Bottom: If you're just starting a roadracing career, remember this: When track-record holders talk, you listen. Scott Gray (left) gave me advice on throttle use at Willow Springs in 1990 that helped me win the AMA 250GP National. (Author's collection)

Right: Abrupt throttle movements make passengers miserable, no matter what you ride or drive. Smoothing and slowing your right hand while riding your bike, or your right foot while driving your car, will make everyone more comfortable.

that's the only way to calm your fingers as they squeeze the brake lever. Snap the throttle shut at low rpm and nothing much happens. Repeat the mistake near redline and you run the risk of locking the rear tire under engine compression, especially if you follow with a stab at the front brake. Begin training your right hand to always move in a controlled, smooth manner. Your destiny rides in your right hand.

TRYING TOO HARD

Street riding can be made more difficult by trying too hard. An overaggressive rider who uses too much throttle must wait for his bike to settle down. During that period the rider isn't accelerating, braking or even steering—no inputs are being made to any of the bike's controls. Meanwhile, the bike is moving forward at what could be a high rate of speed, and the rider finds himself a helpless passenger. At 60 mph, the bike covers 88 feet every second, so an overaggressive move that distracts the rider for half a second could take 44 feet to happen. Do you have 44 feet to wait until your bike settles down?

As your throttle control becomes more adept, with calmer, gentler movements, you'll find your brain is better able to judge cornering speed and braking distances because it is no longer dealing with the panic and distraction of an out-of-control motorcycle. Because you're no longer slamming the throttle shut and grabbing at the front brake, your bike isn't loading up the front tire and suspension while the rear end wags in the breeze. Your brain

becomes free to think about fun subjects like cornering speed, lean angle and bike placement...all because you're closing your throttle, not snapping it shut.

DRILL TIME: GO SLOW-MO

Rolling the throttle off smoothly will take practice, and I don't recommend trying it for the first time while launching yourself toward a corner at 65 mph. Start slower: first gear. Take your bike out on a deserted street or parking lot and accelerate and decelerate in first gear, using various rpm. Roll the throttle on and off slowly at first, just easing it open and easing it closed. Really concentrate on your right hand, finessing the grip open and closed. As you get smoother, increase the rpm and try to roll the throttle on and off just as smoothly, but more quickly. Find the point at which you can quickly open and close the throttle while maintaining smoothness. This skill must be practiced constantly to overcome our inherent instinct to be more aggressive when trying to excel in sports.

Extend this drill into your cars, trucks, dirt bikes—whatever you drive with a throttle. Start paying attention to how you lift off the throttle in your car and how you pick that throttle back up. Get in the habit of never rushing either movement, no matter what you ride or drive. It's vital that you master this and make it part of your vehicle operation because as you begin to go faster (and use more lean angle), loading those tires' contact patches is all about smoothness.

CLOSE BUT NOT CLOSED: REMEMBER MAINTENANCE THROTTLE

A quick review from the previous chapter on steering: You enter a corner off the throttle, with much of the weight of the bike on the front tire as it leans into the corner. If over-loaded, the front tire will lose traction, so you must learn to ease the throttle open just enough to transfer some weight off the front tire, but not enough to actually accelerate the bike. We call this *maintenance throttle.*

The reason for sneaking on the throttle is two-fold. As we discussed in chapter 4, throttle will make the bike cease steering into the corner, so if you turn your bike into the corner and grab some throttle, it will be tough to make the apex. Second, if you grab the throttle at lean angle, it's very possible to overwhelm the rear tire's traction as it deals with cornering and acceleration forces. The crash that results is called a *high-side:* The bike slides sideways, then the tire abruptly grabs traction, stops sliding, and the rider is launched over the high side (which is in the opposite

direction of the bike's original lean angle).

This neutral throttle, or maintenance throttle, will arrest and hold constant the bike's lean angle, unload the front tire slightly, load the rear tire gently and give the bike an amazingly balanced feel. Remember, this isn't accelerating throttle—this is just enough throttle to unload the front tire and maintain the lean angle.

A great bonus of being smooth with the throttle is speed, pure and simple. When the bike isn't bobbing and weaving on its suspension, the rider's brain stays calm and focused on gear selection, entrance speed, tire traction and cornering line. A calm right hand affects many things in a very positive way. It's much easier to judge traction when your bike isn't violently loading and unloading the front or rear tire. As your right hand smooths out its control manipulations, you'll find yourself riding more quickly with a higher degree of comfort.

THE REAR TIRE AND 100 POINTS OF TRACTION

The question of how much traction a motorcycle tire can provide doesn't have a hard-and-fast answer. I wish this book could tell you to enter a freeway on-ramp at 53 mph and lean over to 33 degrees to get to the limit of traction. However, it's this lack of well-defined borders that makes our sport so challenging and enthralling.

Over the years I've come to describe traction levels of

Above: Fast rider, slow right hand. Why? Because this R1's rear tire is busy dealing with lean angle points, so the rider can't afford to add additional acceleration points and risk overwhelming the tire's available traction. This is where maintenance throttle comes in, delivered with a slow right hand. (Brian Blades)

A. and B. The vital importance of maintenance throttle will be clear when you compare the difference in the size of the contact patch loaded (A) and unloaded (B). More rubber on the road equals more traction, so think about sneaking open the throttle to load the rear tire before beginning serious acceleration. (Dennis Morrison)

C. This rear tire can accelerate hard and corner hard, and the secret to exiting a corner safely and consistently is to slowly add acceleration points while you stand the bike up off the corner, reducing lean angle points. Your initial throttle application must be super-slow and smooth because the rear tire's contact patch increases significantly as the bike's weight transfers rearward. Think about pressing the rear tire into the pavement before acceleration, not just snapping on the throttle. (Brian Blades)

tires based on a theoretical 100 points of traction. This 100-point system applies to soft, sticky slicks as well as harder, mileage-biased touring tires because each tire has 100 points of traction at whatever maximum traction level it possesses. As you're riding you can use these 100 traction points in a variety of ways, but you must respect the fact that your tires have only 100 points, and you can't use more than you've got.

For a rear tire, those 100 points are divided between providing acceleration and providing cornering traction. With the bike straight up and down, all 100 points are applied to acceleration traction—in fact, the traction is so good that the bike can wheelie over backward. But as the bike leans into a corner, the same tire's acceleration points are traded for cornering traction points. As the bike gets to full lean and the rear tire is steered onto its edge, most of the traction points are given to cornering traction with very few left for acceleration. But the cornering traction at full lean is still so good that the rider can actually drag his inside knee on the ground. When you stop to think about it, that's pretty incredible.

If the rider leans the bike into a corner and uses 97 points for cornering traction and then asks for 5 points of acceleration traction, something's going to give, and that something can result in a subtle slip or a hard-hitting high-side. The difference is in how the rider approaches or exceeds the 100 available traction points. An aggressive right hand adds acceleration points too quickly, suddenly overwhelming a tire that's already giving 97 of its available

Above: Top left: A production street bike doesn't lean over much farther than this, so it's safe to assume there aren't many traction points left for acceleration. Think about reserving the edges of your rear tire to change the bike's direction at maximum lean angle, not for acceleration. (Jeff Allison)
Right: The more horsepower your bike makes, the more closely you must monitor your acceleration points. Coming up from a full lean on Kenny Roberts Jr.'s 500GP bike, my right hand is just sneaking on the throttle. That light acceleration extends the fork and encourages the bike to stand up off the apex, allowing me to carefully add acceleration points for the diminishing lean angle points. It's safe to add acceleration points if you're giving away lean angle points. (Gold & Goose)

points to cornering. A subtle right hand will be able to ease up to the 100 points with complete confidence and with repeatable results. This subtle right hand either wins road-racing championships or extends a street-riding career, both excellent goals.

The 100 rear tire traction points can be exceeded through a variety of approaches. The example in the preceding paragraph talks about the consequences of leaning the bike over, then stabbing at the throttle and overwhelming the rear tire's ability to maintain traction. But you can also open the throttle first, then lean the bike into the corner and overwhelm the rear tire's ability to stay hooked up; in both cases, the combined points of acceleration and cornering traction add up to over 100, and the tire slides.

Adding lean angle with the throttle open is a frightening thing to watch in a beginning rider. That rider wants to go

Above: Even extremely gifted riders, such as AMA 600 Supersport racer Jake Zemke, can get greedy when balancing throttle and lean angle at a corner exit. When you factor in slippery Daytona pavement and hard compound tires, the need for a slow throttle hand is even more important. (Brian J. Nelson)

Below right: Nicky Hayden's Superbike tire is beginning to "chunk," or separate, where it's being used the hardest. Use the far outside edges of the tire for direction change, not acceleration. Truly hard acceleration should take place as the bike stands up from maximum lean angle, as you are giving back cornering points. (Brian J. Nelson)

How important is it? Let me take you back to 1990, Willow Springs Raceway, Rosamond, California. The AMA nationals had come to town, and I was one of the fast Willow Springs club racers entered in the 250GP class on my Del Amo Yamaha TZ250, tuned by Steve Biganski. After two days of practice, we found ourselves in the hunt for the win, running lap times comparable to the national boys. The night before the race, I had a chance to talk with Scott Gray, the Willow Springs track record holder, and his advice was simple: "Try to pick up the throttle a little bit earlier in every corner." The next day I won my first AMA 250GP national going away. Thanks, Scott.

So the answer to the question of when to start sneaking the throttle open is: Do it as soon as possible after the bike changes direction. The earlier you begin sneaking the throttle open, the smoother and finer you must be on the twist grip, because your rear tire is using most of its 100 points for cornering traction. The farther you lean your bike into the corner, the more gently you must add acceleration. Believe me, the fastest racers in the world have the finest feel in their right hands. They're leaning way over, yet still have enough sensitivity to add the one or two acceleration traction points to keep the rear tire at 100 points of traction. A good way to think about it is this: fast bike, slow hand.

After reaching full lean angle, you'll soon begin standing the bike up to exit the corner. As you stand your bike up off the edge of the tire, acceleration traction points become available as you give back cornering traction points. That means you can roll the throttle open gently and smoothly as the bike stands up off the corner. This answers the question of when to accelerate in a corner: only when you see the exit and can begin to take away lean angle.

faster and automatically thinks the throttle is the answer. Wrong. As you learn more about how a bike works, you realize that this beginning rider is going to have difficulty getting his bike turned. That's because a bike likes to turn with the throttle shut, or at least reduced, to load the front end. Also, this beginning rider risks high-siding as he adds lean angle, which adds cornering points, without reducing acceleration points. He simply needs to let the bike turn into the corner, change direction, with the throttle shut. It doesn't matter whether you add too many acceleration points while leaned over or add too many cornering points while accelerating: Any combination that adds up to over 100 points is going to cause a slide.

PICKING UP THE THROTTLE

After you've rolled the throttle shut smoothly and turned the bike into the corner, it's time to start your drive off the corner by going to maintenance throttle to arrest and hold the bike's lean angle. Imagine the slightest turn of the throttle, just easing it up off the idle stop. Imagine the throttle cables just barely tightening up. Imagine moving the carburetor slides or fuel-injection throttle bodies just a fraction of a hair. Imagine just trickling some fuel into the combustion chamber, because that's the type of throttle feel that the best riders in the world possess. I've tried to say it in many ways because it's that important.

One way to think about trading cornering traction points for accelerating points as the bike stands up off the corner is by imagining that there's a wire connecting your right wrist and the rear tire's contact patch. When the bike is on the side of the tire, at full lean, the wire can pull the rider's wrist open only a little bit. As the tire rolls toward the middle and the bike stands up, the wire can pull the wrist downward, opening the throttle in small increments until the bike is straight up and down and the throttle is wide open. Now, you won't use wide-open throttle much on the street, but when you do, thinking about this wire connecting your right wrist and the rear tire contact patch will make your acceleration much safer.

It's entirely possible to open the throttle too early. The secret to correct throttle application is to allow the bike to steer into the corner off-throttle and wait until the bike has pointed itself into the corner before you sneak the throttle open. A sure sign that a rider is accelerating too soon is that the bike continues to run wide in slow corners. The rider gets impatient because the corner is slow, pulls the throttle open, and that action extends the fork and lets the bike run wide. Keep that throttle shut until the bike is steered in, and then begin easing it open.

100 POINTS IN THE RAIN

Rain, gravel, slick cement—none of these actually take away any of your 100 traction points but they do lower the scale. In the rain, your rear tire will still provide a combination of 100 points split between cornering and acceleration, but that 100-point scale is nowhere near the 100 points you can expect from the same tires on dry asphalt. Reduced traction simply means it will take less lean angle and less throttle to reach the limits of adhesion, but it's still a combination of the two that must be respected. Rain means slower hands and less-abrupt steering inputs, the same things the fastest racers think about while approaching the limits of adhesion in the dry.

It is the same story with old, used tires. You can still combine cornering and acceleration (or cornering and braking up front), but your 100-point scale is significantly lower than it was when the tires were new. As you learn and respect this 100-point scale, it becomes clear why some of the fastest roadracers in the world are also some of the most consistent roadracers in the world. Your tires will only give so much, and when it comes to the rear tire, the secret is right there in your throttle hand.

THROTTLE DRILL

On your next ride, roll off the throttle in slow motion the very first time you need to decelerate. Take lots of time and distance to slowly shut the throttle, completely focusing on the smooth,

Above: This Super Motard rider spins the tire at the corner exit to help finish the turn and aim the bike down the next straight, adding throttle points as he takes away lean angle points. Riding a dirt bike makes the throttle/lean angle/traction relationship very clear. (Brian Blades)
Below: Miguel DuHamel smokes the rear tire of his RC51 off Daytona's turn one. Notice how upright the Honda is, allowing Miguel to control the spin by steering, throttle control and body English (using his weight and position to control the bike). But trying to spin it this hard at maximum lean angle could result in a painful "high-side" crash, in which the rear tire breaks loose, the bike goes sideways, and the rear tire regains traction and throws the rider over the top of the bike. The AMA's winningest Superbike rider understands the balance between throttle and lean angle. (Brian J. Nelson)

slow rotation of the throttle. Get your brain focused on your right hand.

Pay special attention to how quickly your right hand moves. If you slam off the throttle, you will almost surely grab at the brake. Focus on rolling off the throttle smoothly and notice how it smooths the transition to braking.

You should also pay special attention to how quickly the front end dives under deceleration. If you chop the throttle quickly, the front end will drop correspondingly. If you ease off

These guys roadrace (guess which one is Nicky Hayden), but small dirt bikes allow them to practice exceeding the limits of traction without ugly consequences. Throttle control may be the most valuable skill for both racers and street bike riders. (Jeff Allen)

the throttle, notice how much more smoothly the front moves.

While riding at highway speeds, try different gears to experience how much more difficult it is to manipulate the throttle smoothly at higher rpm. In top gear, the throttle response is relatively sluggish when compared to third gear at the same speed. It's fairly easy to be smooth when the engine's not making much power, but the real challenge is maintaining that smoothness at high rpm.

Listen to your bike's drive chain as you accelerate and decelerate in top gear. Can you hear it clunk? Try and smooth your right hand's movements until your bike's drive chain can no longer be heard.

GIVE IT A BLIP

The throttle has another use, apart from speed control and cornering assistance. A small on/off twist of the throttle (a *blip*) can be used to help smooth a downshift, or even an upshift. This blip comes as the clutch is squeezed and the new gear selected, as the engine is freed from the transmission by the clutch. The engine is free to rev, so a quick blip brings the engine speed up, preventing it from falling to idle during the gear change.

Blipping your engine during a downshift takes a bit of practice, but the results are smooth gear changes and substantially less wear on your clutch. Each and every downshift should get a blip, whether you're riding a bike or driving a car. If it doesn't, you'll be putting a clutch in sooner rather than later. Besides saving the clutch and making your passenger a lot more comfortable, blipping sounds cool. We'll talk more about it in chapter 6.

LESSONS FROM THE RACETRACK

RESPECTING THE CHANGING EDGE OF TRACTION If the fastest roadracers in the world are winning races, they must be taking the most chances, right? Yet national and international champions rarely fall off their bikes. That's because these pros not only understand the concept of lean angle versus throttle that we covered above, but also *how it changes over the course of a race.* At full lean, the rear tire has few, if any, points left for acceleration. As the tire ages during a race, that 100-point scale (divisible between cornering and acceleration traction) slides downward, and a winning rider's throttle control must improve.

EARLY, SMOOTH THROTTLE APPLICATION If a racer can pick up the throttle 10 feet before his competitor does, that racer can effectively lengthen the adjoining straight. Accelerating sooner means more speed, and a racer who picks up the throttle early is often accused of having a faster bike when the straightaway speeds are measured. The more revealing measurement is speed just past the apex of a corner.

RELATIVELY PAINLESS PRACTICE Roadracers constantly search for ways to improve their throttle control because it is the secret to balancing rear tire traction. Many of these riders have turned to dirt track racing (or playing) on bikes like Honda's XR line. A few hours spent sliding around a muddy oval with your friends is a darn good time, and few can deny the benefits to their roadracing efforts. Be sure to wear pads: More roadracers get hurt dirt bike riding than roadracing!

DON'T TRY TOO HARD WITH THE THROTTLE Back when I was racing at Willow Springs every month, occasionally I would hear a rider complain about losing rear tire traction in turn two, a sweeping fourth-gear right-hander. It was invariably a slower rider complaining. What was happening? The rider would enter the turn a bit too slowly, then realize he could go faster and nail the throttle to accelerate. Since the rear tire was already leaned over a good way (let's say the rear tire was using 80 points of cornering traction), the sudden burst of acceleration (let's say 25 points of acceleration traction) was simply too much. Faster riders would get in the same corner and simply ease the throttle open, sneaking up to the rear tire's 100 available traction points.

BIG BLIPS Roadracers without slipper clutches (a mechanism that reduces the effects of engine deceleration) can't afford to have the rear tire lock up momentarily at a corner entrance due to a rough downshift, so they work hard on mastering the art of braking and blipping while downshifting. Street riders have even less room for mistakes, so practice this skill until it's second nature. Read more about blipping in chapter 6.

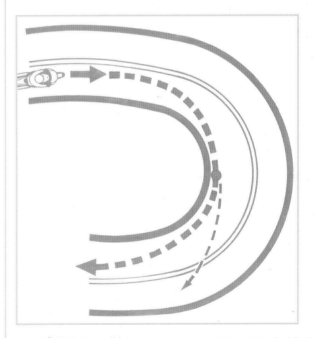

Above: In this illustration the rider does a good job turning the bike into the corner, but the thin dotted line shows the problems that come from aggressive mid-corner acceleration. Abrupt acceleration encourages the bike to stand up, and that puts it across the centerline in this long corner. The thick dotted line shows the proper line and emphasizes the importance of allowing the bike to turn through the corner, then easing on the throttle only after you see the exit. (Hector Cademartori)

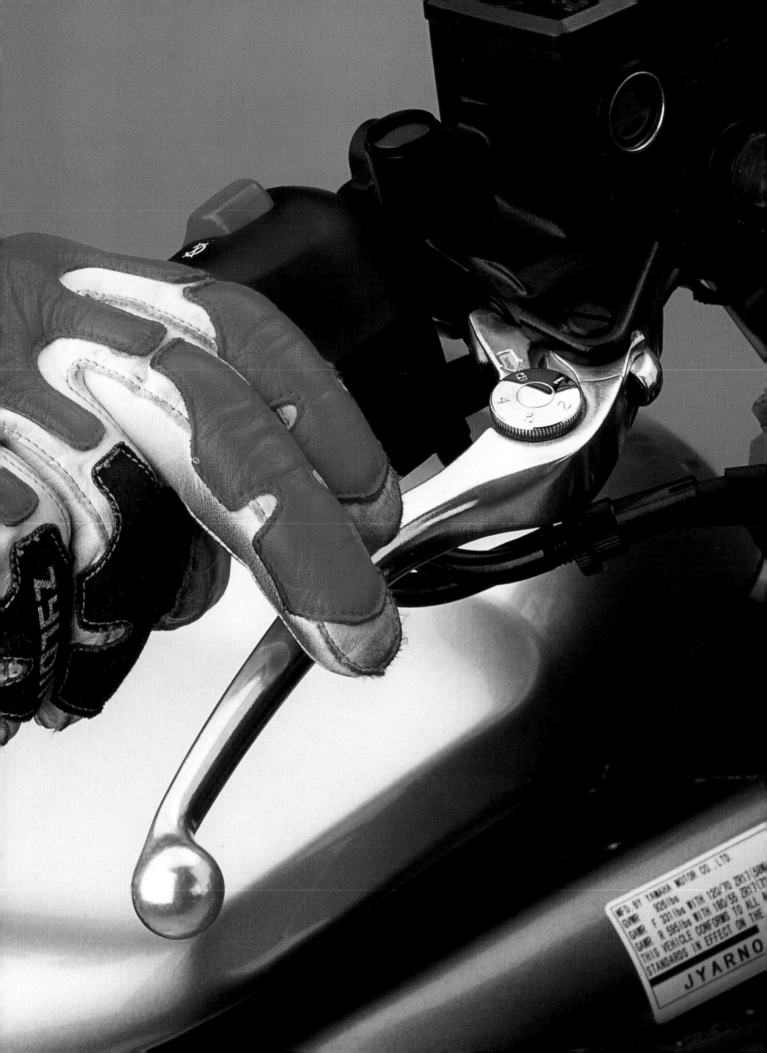

CHAPTER 6

BRAKES

A MOTORCYCLE'S MOST POWERFUL COMPONENT DOES MUCH MORE THAN JUST STOP

If you're looking for one riding skill to truly master, choose braking. Using the brakes well will not only make every ride more enjoyable, but it may save your ass. Once again, your right hand is the focal point when it comes to improving your braking skills. Your right index and middle fingers control your destiny, with the right foot contributing as well. The training and control of the right hand and foot ranks second only to that of the brain when building a good motorcycle rider.

Compared to the "skill" of acceleration, the skill of braking is significantly more difficult. Just ask the thousands of riders who have accelerated down a straight road only to find themselves unable to shed their velocity in time for the upcoming corner. Good brake usage is paramount for every rider on public roads.

YOUR BUDDY, THE BRAKES

You must find the time not only to study this difficult skill, but also to practice aboard your bike in a controlled setting. Sure, you say to yourself, I need a bit of practice, and someday I'll find a clear road or parking lot and do a few stops. The only problem with this approach is that emergencies rarely happen according to our schedules. So the sooner you improve your braking skills, the more prepared you'll be for the next emergency. It might be tomorrow afternoon. Are you ready?

I've observed many riders try unsuccessfully to stop their bikes. All of these riders could accelerate well, but when it came to curbing their speed, the difference in stopping distances was as varied as the types of motorcycle ridden. The bikes had almost nothing to do with the variance. It all came down to the fingers squeezing the brakes and the minds operating the fingers. As with all rider inputs, the name of the game is smoothness. Apply the brakes gradually, feel the transfer of weight to the front, and then really increase the pressure that you apply to the front and rear

brakes. The process needs to happen quickly and in a controlled manner. Squeeze the front brake lever—don't grab it.

Having witnessed these variations in braking skills, I understand why many crashes occur within two months of buying a new bike. Every bike has unique braking characteristics, and if you haven't taken time to familiarize yourself with the way your bike stops, ugly things can happen.

BRAKE TESTING

This chapter's observations, hints and tips about braking are inspired by my experience watching and participating in braking tests. Like you, I've always realized the importance of being able to stop a motorcycle well, but it wasn't until I

Left: A motorcycle's forward weight transfer during braking makes the front tire the workhorse, whether it's an emergency or you're simply slowing for a red light. A refined touch on the brake lever will save you in an emergency and improve your bike's handling during every ride. (Brian Blades)

Below: Many of us have more than one bike. This rider tours on his Triumph Sprint but rides a GSX-R600 in the canyons. Those two bikes have decidedly different braking characteristics, so their owner must constantly reacquaint himself with both through braking practice. (Brian Blades)

invited a group of riders to a parking lot in Torrance, California, for a story on braking for *Motorcyclist* magazine that I appreciated how much more difficult motorcycles are to stop than cars. Rider skill at the front brake lever was significantly more important than the model of bike, brand of tire or brake pad compound when it came to separating those who could consistently stop a motorcycle in a short distance from those who simply grabbed and hoped. I saw riders who were scared of the brakes, ignorant of the brakes' strength, overconfident in their braking abilities—yet all of them were able to accelerate their motorcycle just fine. Dealing with the speed that followed proved to be the tougher challenge.

We assembled eight riders of various abilities in a huge, clean parking lot. We asked the riders to accelerate their motorcycles to 40 mph, and then stop the bike when they passed an orange cone. The morning began on a terrible note when the very first participant rode toward the cone at 40 mph and upon passing it, grabbed the front brake lever like a kid reaching for an ice cream cone. The front tire locked, skidded sideways and threw the rider down, breaking his collarbone. It was a harsh demonstration of that tremendously important braking tip: Squeeze the front brake lever—don't grab it.

As the morning wore on, I saw one rider concentrating so hard on the brakes that he forgot to shut the throttle. Another rider continually locked the rear brake, which then scared her into releasing both brakes and, of course, lengthening her stopping distances. All morning long, the remaining seven riders circled and stopped, circled and stopped. By noon, the stops were shorter, more controlled and repeatable, and each showed significant improvement. The shorter stopping distances also led each rider to express greater confidence in their braking abilities.

Only one of these eight licensed riders had been practicing their stops every week, but they all left resolved to develop the habit of practicing. That's because they had seen, first hand, what a morning of practice can do. And they weren't the only ones. After getting an eyeful of what can happen when a rider isn't friends with the brakes, I left that parking lot wanting to practice—a lot.

BUT PRACTICE WHAT?

If you were to speak to a marksman, he would talk about *squeezing* the gun's trigger, not *pulling* the trigger. Let's take that analogy into our braking practice and get in the habit of squeezing the front brake lever, not grabbing it.

Above: It's not surprising that the rear brake is so easy to abuse given the difficulty of developing feel through a heavy boot. Protective riding boots are necessary, but if your first attempt to use the rear brake is in an emergency, you'll definitely lock it up. So P-R-A-C-T-I-C-E! (Brian Blades)

Left: This front brake system is designed to repeatedly stop a 430-pound bike from 160 mph, yet with the right touch it offers tremendous sensitivity and feel. In this case, the software—you—must be developed to match the hardware's capabilities.

That initial squeeze is the equivalent of sneaking the throttle open to begin the corner exit, allowing the bike to settle back on that rear tire before true acceleration really begins. By squeezing the front brake lever to begin the braking process, you allow the motorcycle's weight to transfer smoothly to the front end, compressing the fork slightly and loading the tire. After this initial smooth squeeze, the brakes can be applied with vigor. Without the initial squeeze, the forward weight shift can be too violent. In fact, grab the brake too aggressively and the front tire can lock before the bike's weight has a chance to shift forward. Beating the weight transfer like this will immediately lock the tire and perhaps lead to a crash. To help remember to squeeze, you can play with the spelling of *weight*: "Wait on the weight transfer."

Spend time and thought on squeezing the front brake lever, and make it a habit every time you go to the brakes. Stopping a motorcycle isn't always done on perfect pavement, and it isn't always done in a straight line. If you gradually squeeze the front brake lever toward the bar, stopping in rain or mid-corner (or in the middle of a rainy corner) will be a much less adrenaline-filled affair. If your tendency is to grab and stab at the front brake lever, a low-traction condition will eventually catch you out, and you will fall.

FINDING THE THRESHOLD OF LOCK-UP

After the initial squeeze, bear down on the brake lever and get a feel for how well your bike stops. Listen for the tire to talk to you, because at maximum deceleration the front tire will howl slightly. The main technique you should master is attaining a total focus on the pressure of your right-hand fingers. As your confidence improves, you will be able to either skid the front tire momentarily or allow the rear end of your bike to lift off the ground, depending upon the bike you're riding. Bikes with longer wheelbases and more relaxed steering geometry will skid the front tire, while shorter, more aggressive sport bikes will lift the rear tire as the front approaches lock-up. When either occurs, immediately but smoothly release pressure on the brake lever, and train yourself to release only enough pressure to unlock the wheel or lower the back end. If you get scared and completely release the brake lever, your braking distances will be significantly longer.

What you're experimenting with is *threshold braking,* or braking to the verge of locking the wheels. This is the outer limit of straight-line braking, and I suggest you become comfortable there.

When applying the rear brake, use the toes of your right foot on the brake pedal, and use them lightly, with as much feel as you can muster. The secret to the rear brake is "use it, don't abuse it." A locked rear brake, especially in a corner, is distracting at best and contributes to a crash at worst. Make sure to leave the heel of your foot on the foot peg and simply flex the ankle forward and down. If you take your foot off the peg and place it on the brake pedal, you can easily lose feel, and the brake can immediately lock. We'll discuss the rear brake in more depth later in this chapter.

Setting Speed Precisely: Trail-braking

Trail-braking's bottom line is safety. The ability to trail-brake allows you to set your cornering speed closer to the apex, which is the slowest point in the corner. Those who use their brakes in a straight line and then let go of them to steer their bikes are deciding very early in the corner what speed they need. If you always ride the same road, this technique works okay—as long as there are no mid-corner surprises. But the ability to use your brakes leaned over will allow speed adjustments all the way through the corner, even past the apex if necessary. Remember: The faster you ride, the more you will use your brakes. That means earlier application and more pressure over a longer distance.

Braking Practice Credo

If you ride at 120 mph, you had better practice braking from 120 mph. Find a place to do a few high-speed emergency stops; that experiment will open your eyes to the difficulty of stopping a bike from high speed. The distance it takes to stop your bike may have you rethinking your Sunday morning speed.

Left: As a matter of vehicle dynamics, a motorcycle slows when you turn it, but to set your entrance speed efficiently and with repeatable results, use the component designed for that purpose: the brakes. (Brian Blades)

Right: This front tire can brake hard and corner hard. Once you begin treating your front brake lever as a rheostat, not an on/off switch, you will be comfortable squeezing on the brakes at lean angle. And what about getting into a corner too hot? Let's say this tire has 100 points of lean angle and is using 86 of those points for cornering. A smooth right hand can add 14 braking points in an emergency, while an abrupt hand would grab 40 points and fall down. (Brian Blades)

Below: Every corner has its slowest point. In this 180-degree turn, the slowest point comes well into the turn, about three-quarters of the way through. To ensure your speed at the slowest point, learn to use the brakes while leaned over. This diagram shows how brake pressure must diminish as lean angle is added, and how throttle pressure can increase as lean angle is taken away. Imagine how tough this would be if the rider has an abrupt right hand. Be smooth. (Hector Cademartori)

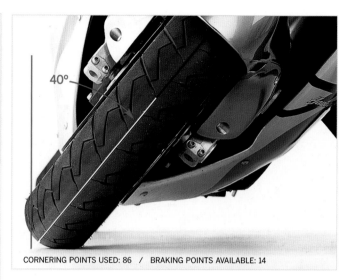

CORNERING POINTS USED: 86 / BRAKING POINTS AVAILABLE: 14

THE FRONT TIRE AND THE 100 POINTS OF TRACTION

Remember the 100 points of tire traction? In a straight line, with the motorcycle fully upright, the front tire can handle tremendous braking forces. In fact, the front tire will stop so hard that many sport bikes can actually rotate over forward in a "stoppie." Application of the front brake transfers the bike's weight forward, and as the fork collapses, the tire is loaded even more. That makes for amazing stopping power, and in the example of a stoppie, you can see that all 100 points of traction go to braking when traveling in a straight line.

Now, as the bike leans into a corner, some of the braking traction points will be traded for cornering traction points. Maybe only a few at first, but as the bike continues to lean into the turn, more of the tire's 100 available points are being used to maintain cornering traction, so the rider must ease off the brake lever to fill the growing need for cornering traction points. This technique is called trail-braking, or trailing the brakes off as the bike enters the corner. If the rider continues to brake hard while leaning the bike into the turn, the 100 available traction points, split between braking and cornering, will be exceeded. And when you run out of traction points, the tire slides.

It's the way you approach 100 traction points that makes the difference between a slide and a complete loss of traction, or a crash. If the rider takes the tire to 100 points in small, progressive steps, the slide is often quite controllable. If the rider jumps to the limit (or beyond) in an aggression-filled instant, traction is suddenly overwhelmed and used up. Anyone who has tried to force a bike to turn while at maximum braking is familiar with the bike's resistance to turning when

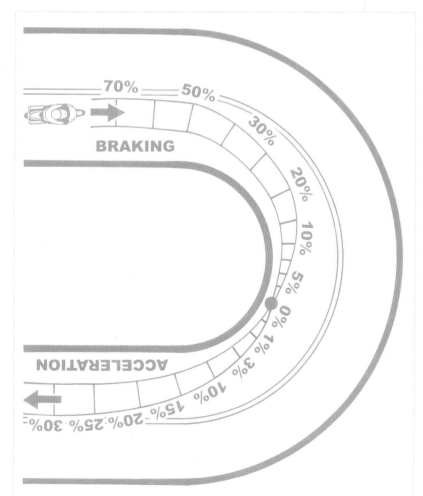

70% — 50%

30%

20%

10%

5%

0%

BRAKING

ACCELERATION

1% 1% 3% 5% 10% 15% 20% 25% 30%

braking traction will be available to you. The key is applying the brakes gradually so you avoid exceeding the 100 points and losing the front end.

As your bike slows, it requires less lean angle for the given corner radius, and less lean angle (with fewer cornering traction points) allows you to add braking traction points because the bike can stand up. Use this simple equation: Radius Equals Miles per Hour. Dropping your speed tightens up the bike's radius, which allows you to take away lean angle and still stay in your lane. But the most important step in this scenario is your ability to go to your front and rear brakes smoothly and controllably. Trail-braking is the answer to the question: What if I get in the corner too hot? Keep your eyes focused on where you want the bike to go, and continue to trail-brake. As your speed comes down, your radius will tighten, allowing you to stand the bike up—that means you can brake even harder. Never give up on the brakes when your entrance speed is too high.

the front suspension is bottomed. You need to give away braking points to allow the front suspension to rebound slightly, and then the bike can turn more easily. Think of it as trading braking points for the cornering points you are adding.

At this point, the rider must not simply let go of the front brake lever. First, the bike's speed might not yet be set for the corner. Second, completely letting go of the front brake lever allows the fork to rebound completely, and the bike won't be as eager to turn due to the extended geometry. The rider should *ease* off the brakes as the bike is turned into the corner, allowing her fingers to give away braking points as the bike rolls in toward maximum lean angle. A fine feel on the brake lever is needed because the rider is balancing braking and cornering points, keeping the front tire from exceeding 100 total points. The rider is trading the braking forces that compressed the front suspension for cornering forces that compress the front suspension, and when it's done right, it's the epitome of smoothness.

TRAIL-BRAKING NEEDS SMOOTH HANDS

Once you begin trailing your brakes into the corners, you will be convinced that a tire can handle the combination of braking and cornering. That's an important concept to realize, because someday you will be surprised by a mid-corner emergency. If you're leaned into a corner at 84 points, you still have 16 points left for braking. And if you're in the habit of squeezing the front brake lever and loading the front tire smoothly, there's a good chance those 16 points of

Above: Jimmy Filice made few mistakes on a 250, but this classic low-side was due to one thing: too much front brake pressure for the bike's lean angle. New tires, cold tires, cold racetrack—all may have contributed to the lack of traction, but the lesson for street riders is this: Err on the side of safety by setting corner entrance speed early and not relying on heavy trail-braking deep into a turn. You have no runoff room on public highways if you get it wrong. (Brian J. Nelson)

Below: Adjustability is a wonderful thing, because no two riders are identical. Be sure your brake and clutch levers are positioned so your fingers can rest on them comfortably, which means well below the handgrip on most sport bikes. And since modern brakes rarely fade, this lever is being adjusted via the five-position wheel to give maximum feel while trail-braking. (Brian Blades)

BRAKES AND A BLIP

As you discovered in chapter 2, the basics of motorcycle control serve to keep the bike between the lines, but it's the more advanced skills that make this sport so incredible. Most riders can downshift and most riders can brake, but the tough part comes when you combine the two skills. After all, you don't want to sacrifice your braking just because you've got to pop a few downshifts, yet you don't want to ignore the necessary downshifts because you're on the brakes, right? Again, it's the right hand that controls these two actions.

The purpose of a downshift is to put the engine in the proper rpm range for the future, whether it's the upcoming corner exit, hill or pass. So even as you're braking for a corner, you need to learn to downshift at the same time. One of the first things they teach you at automotive driving schools is a technique called the *heel and toe,* in which the driver uses the toes of his right foot on the brake pedal while simultaneously using the heel or side of the same foot to boot the accelerator. Doing both at once allows you to match revs for the lower gear. Matching revs is just as important on a motorcycle as it is in a car, since it helps you make seamlessly smooth downshifts and reduces wear on the clutch plates.

If you've taken my advice to use two fingers on the front brake lever, then the remaining two fingers and thumb will be wrapped around the throttle grip to turn, or *blip,* the throttle on the downshift. The tough part is maintaining constant pressure on the front brake lever while blipping the throttle. On your first few attempts, you'll find yourself pulling and

A properly executed downshift is often necessary while braking, so we must learn to "blip" (rev) the throttle as the clutch is disengaged and the lower gear selected, while slowing the bike with the brakes. The blip matches the engine speed to the new gear, making for a seamless downshift without the jerkiness of a "blipless" downshift. The steps are physically easy, but relatively tough to coordinate at first.

A. Close the throttle and squeeze on the front brake. You never want to accelerate and brake at the same time, so make sure that throttle is shut. **B.** Pull in the clutch, but use only two fingers and use your ring finger as a clutch-lever limiter because the clutch lever doesn't need to be pulled all the way to the bar for a shift. **C.** Make your downshift with a controlled movement of the shift lever, don't kick at it. **D.** Blip your throttle (a short rev) while continuing to brake and while the clutch lever is still pulled in. **E.** Let out the clutch lever in a controlled manner, just in case you haven't matched the rpm perfectly to the new gear. If you have four downshifts to execute for a corner, that means a total of four clutch movements and four blips (one of each per gear) because a sequential transmission likes to be reloaded between shifts. (Brian Blades)

Tips for practicing: Letting the clutch lever out too quickly is one of two reasons your downshift will be rough. The other is that your blip didn't send the rpm high enough for the new gear. Steps 1 through 5 happen almost simultaneously when the downshift is done correctly.

releasing the brake lever. This creates a pogoing front fork assembly during downshifts, but stick with it. Whatever you do, don't quit trying to blip the throttle on the downshifts while braking, because botching a downshift while slightly leaned over can momentarily lock the rear tire, and that's the last thing you want to have happen. Any time you hear the rear tire chirp as you release the clutch lever after a downshift, it's a sign that the rpm wasn't correctly matched, and that the spinning rear tire locked momentarily as it dragged the engine up to speed. Rather than depending upon the rear tire, chain, clutch, crankshaft and connecting rods to get your engine to the right rpm, give the throttle a blip while you have the clutch in, to match the engine rpm with the newly selected gear. Time your clutch re-engagement to take best advantage of the blip, allowing the lower gear to be selected smoothly and consistently.

Most bikes offer an adjustable front brake lever, so take advantage of this design by placing the brake lever where it works best for your hand size. I've noticed that many riders adjust their brake levers a bit too far away from the throttle, robbing them of feel and strength during tricky braking maneuvers.

Braking and downshifting simultaneously isn't difficult from a skills perspective, but it is difficult from a timing perspective. The goal is to bring the engine up to speed using the throttle while the clutch is disengaged and the downshift is being made. If you grab and release the clutch abruptly, the downshift will suffer, so remember to use two fingers on the clutch. Also, bring the lever in just far enough to make contact with your ring finger. Remember to release that clutch smoothly and control the lever all the way out, because it is your final safety net in the downshift procedure. If you accidentally downshift twice, or are unsure of which gear you are in, the habit of letting the clutch engage smoothly will be a lifesaver.

COMING TO TERMS WITH THE REAR BRAKE

Ah yes, the rear brake. The obvious problem in using the rear brake is weight transfer, right? As the front brake is applied, the bike transfers weight forward onto the front tire and off the rear tire. With less weight on the rear tire, the rear brake becomes increasingly touchy and prone to locking. On the most aggressively designed sport bikes, the rear tire can actually leave the ground under hard braking, and you can guess how much pedal pressure it then takes to lock that rear brake: almost none. It's clear why many riders never touch the rear brake.

But studies prove that a combination of front and rear braking will stop a bike more quickly and in less distance than just using the front brake. Many riders have found that applying the rear brake nanoseconds before the front brake

helps settle the bike because the rear suspension isn't so eager to rebound, a trait that helps reduce the forward weight transfer. Because they have longer wheelbases and can be used to carry passengers, many non-sport bikes have extremely usable rear brake systems. So from a functional point of view, it's a good idea to educate your right foot on the pedal.

TEST IT YOURSELF

Get your motorcycle and a friend together to try this experiment to illustrate the rear brake's stabilizing effect. Set the

Above: A mid-corner touch of rear brake helps hold the bike's line down to the apex, shedding that last bit of speed without upsetting the chassis. It's especially easy in a left-hand corner but will require preparing your foot position at the corner entrance. Right-hand turns are trickier because you could catch your foot on the pavement. (Dennis Morrison)

Left: This shot clearly illustrates why riders crash when they panic mid-corner. Too much rear brake plus lean angle means the bike goes sideways. The rear brake can be used, but not abused. (Jeff Allen)

bike's rebound at the softest damping setting possible, and then bounce the rear of the bike while your buddy holds the handlebar. Do it a few times to get an idea of how quickly the rear rebounds upward after you shove on it. Now have your friend apply the rear brake when the rear suspension is being bottomed with your push. If he applies the rear brake at the instant the rear suspension is at maximum compression, you'll notice the rear rebounds more slowly due to the brake's torque reaction against the swingarm and chassis. The application of the rear brake, the caliper clamping the disc, slows the rear shock's rebound as the weight transfers forward by compressing the fork. I know plenty of riders who use the rear brake only for this reaction because it increases control under braking and lessens the abruptness of front-end dive.

USE IT, BUT LIGHTLY

The big trouble comes when riders stomp on the rear brake as if it's a car brake pedal. This stomp often comes at the entrance of a corner, when a rider's overwhelmed brain decides the bike is going too fast. The result is a single black line leading off the pavement, and another story about "running her in there too hot." Too bad, because a soft touch on that rear brake is a great way to shed speed at a corner entrance—and it's an especially great way to adjust speed mid-corner.

That's right, correctly using the rear brake mid-corner is a great way to scrub speed safely. A touch of rear brake

slows the bike well without throwing the weight forward, which would happen if you squeezed the front brake lever. Weight will transfer forward even when using the rear brake, but the fork compression and tire loading will be decidedly different, and safer. This light touch on the rear brake helps drop the bike into the corner—but I emphasize that finesse is needed from the right foot.

In the years I've tested and raced bikes, there have been several times when I couldn't use the rear brake. Once it was because the builder of the bike had fitted a carbon-carbon rear brake disc just for looks and hadn't bothered to make the rear binder functional. Once a flubbed endurance-race pit stop left me with no rear brake pads, while another instance involved a misaligned rear caliper hanger that had prematurely worn out the inside brake pad and forced the caliper into the disc. In every instance, I felt out of control under hard braking because the rear end seemed to wag like a dog's tail as the fork compressed. It was as if the entire motorcycle was balanced on its nose, and I was hesitant turning the bike into the corner because of the fuzzy traction information coming from the rear. When trail-braking into the corner, I found myself missing the comfort of that rear brake and the extra chassis control it afforded. My riding style had adapted to using the rear brake, and when it was missing, I felt its loss.

I kept my rear-brake fondness to myself until a conversation one day with noted roadracing tuner Scotty Beach. While discussing technology, I admitted being hooked on my rear brake. Beach nodded and told me about a little experiment he did with racer Kurt Hall. Kurt is retired now, but you will never forget him if you happened to see him win all three Suzuki Cup races at the WERA Grand National Final in 1992. Hall's championships include national endurance and sprint racing triumphs, and his expertise makes Beach's experiment that much more interesting. One day Beach was touting the pluses of using the rear brake, and Hall, a racer who never used his right foot for anything but balancing on the foot peg, finally gave in and began experimenting with it. As his right-foot skill improved, his lap times tumbled. From that day on, Hall has used his rear brake. No matter what they say, most of the fastest roadracers in the world use that rear binder. Mick Doohan, the five-time 500GP world champion, even developed a thumb brake when his right ankle was immo-

Left: Many enthusiasts can't wait to modify their bikes, and part of that customization is tailoring the controls to fit the rider. Here the rear brake lever is being lowered to require more ankle movement before lock-up, which will help avoid the risk of locking and abusing the rear brake. Don't forget to adjust your rear brake light actuator, too. (Brian Blades)
Above right: Brake manufacturers spend as much time developing brake feel as they do outright power, and it's the improvement in feel that allows 600 Supersport racers to make fast, controlled corner entrances like this. (Brian J. Nelson)

Anti-lock brake systems, or ABS, appeared on motorcycles in the '80s and immediately removed the inherent danger of hard braking in less-than-perfect conditions. I remember flying to Berlin to test the ABS-equipped BMW K100. What sticks with me is the incredible leap of faith we journalists made as we accelerated toward the sand trap BMW had spread out on an airport runway. We began braking on asphalt and then continued into the sand with the brakes mashed on. This was absolutely terrifying the first few times, with heart rates approaching meltdown. But ABS worked, cycling the calipers to eliminate wheel lock-up, and we survived to appreciate the technology.

bile. If the rear brake is no big deal, why did Honda design a thumb brake for Mick?

IS THIS SLICK?

The rear brake makes an excellent traction sampler during straight-line riding. Learn to apply it and then increase the pressure until it locks momentarily, telling you how much traction a particular road surface is offering. When it starts raining, I often use the rear brake to gauge the traction. It's a quick and safe way to get to know a piece of new pavement or to test traction during adverse conditions. You'll develop a feel for how the rear wheel locks and slides, including the sound it produces, which will help your riding considerably. This little pavement test must be done with the bike completely upright and at sane speeds, and the rear tire should remain locked only momentarily to avoid the problem of the rear end sliding to one side or the other. If you squeeze down on the rear brake pedal smoothly, the impending lock-up will give you a huge amount of traction information.

Locking the rear brake can and will happen, and there are two ways to deal with it. The first is to immediately reduce the pressure at the brake pedal before the locked tire slides left or right. The second method is to leave the brake locked and simply steer the front wheel slightly to compensate for the locked rear wheel; if you gently steer straight, the bike will come to a stop and you'll stay upright. In an all-out panic stop, a locked rear brake might be the least of your worries as you modulate the front and try to steer to a safe spot. However, an unlocked rear tire and a skillful right foot will actually prove more helpful in stopping your bike in the shortest distance, so educate that foot and practice threshold braking.

Those first ABS versions gave way to improved technology that cycled more quickly, which shortened the time the system spent releasing the brakes and shortened the stopping distances. Should you buy ABS? Absolutely, because even under perfect conditions (warm and smooth asphalt with hot tires), the rider must be awfully good at stopping to beat the electronic systems.

Manufacturers are also experimenting with linked brake systems, which allow the rear brake pedal to operate a portion of both the front and rear calipers, while the front brake lever does the same. Remember Kurt Hall's experiment? Linked brakes allow you to pull the brake lever and realize the stabilizing effect of a small amount of applied rear brake. The bike will feel more settled at the corner entrance, and you'll have a fine touch for modulation because your fingers are doing the work. If you want maximum braking, you'll have to bring your right foot into play, but for everyday riding, commuting and sport riding, linking the front and rear brakes to the brake lever will add a degree of balance.

LEVERING THE RATIOS

It pays to take some steps to optimize your bike's rear brake, since the engineers couldn't personally fit it to you. First of all, lower the rear brake pedal in relationship to the right foot peg so your ankle will be closer to maximum extension. This position will reduce the leverage and strength of your ankle, putting less pressure on the brake pedal. But be careful not to adjust the brake pedal too low, or it may drag on the ground during cornering. And don't forget to adjust your brake light switch as well.

If rear brake lock-up continues to be a problem after you've adjusted the pedal, you can consider reducing the

mechanical efficiency of the rear brake pads by reducing their swept area, which means the amount of brake rotor area being acted upon by the brake pads. To do so, you can either reduce the amount of disc the pads squeeze or reduce the amount of pad material in the calipers. Teams racing in AMA Supersport competition machine huge holes in their rear discs, or cut away pad material. If this sounds a bit too complicated for you, have a shop do the work. If you've got the money to buy a smaller caliper or a smaller caliper/rotor combination, this is a case where less is definitely better. Whether you reduce the disc's swept area or the size of the brake pads, the rear brake will be less touchy and more useable. Remember, for our sport riding purposes, the rear brake isn't primarily for stopping, it's more for making minute speed corrections and adding stability. If it locks, it's worthless.

The importance of mastering the rear brake pales in comparison to the importance of mastering the front brake. Using the front brake proficiently will save your life due to the forward weight transfer a motorcycle realizes while braking. But a fine touch on the rear brake will make your ride more perfect, while helping you slow your motorcycle better in all conditions. That fine touch will add stability to the motorcycle in the braking zone and will give you additional comfort while braking in less-than-perfect conditions.

LESSONS FROM THE RACETRACK

SQUEEZE, THEN BUILD PRESSURE While slowing for a corner, the best racers do the majority of their braking early in the braking zone, and that means building lever pressure quickly once the bike's weight has transferred onto the front tire. With this hard initial braking, the racer can then fine-tune his or her speed in the last portion of the braking zone, trailing off the brake lever as lean angle is added.

SET YOUR SPEED EXACTLY Racers treat the brake lever not just as a way to stop, but as a speed-setting device that they can manipulate all the way to the apex of the corner if necessary. Trail-braking helps a rider to recover from too much entrance speed, a missed downshift or any other problem at the corner entrance. Being able to control your speed all the way into the corner will get you to the apex every lap, whether you're in traffic or all alone.

UNCONTAMINATED ROTORS As mentioned in chapter 2, racing tuners often clean brake pad deposits off the discs by lightly glass-beading, lightly sanding, or using electrical contact cleaner on the discs. They do this every weekend.

GET UP TO TEMP SLOWLY Brake pads have a tendency to "glaze," or surface-harden, if used too aggressively when new, so racing tuners often put a "new pads" sticker on the tachometer to remind aggressive racers to carefully scrub in the brake pads.

YOU WANT LESS POWER Supersport tuners machine huge holes in the rear brake rotors to lighten them and reduce the grip of the rear brake. Racers can't use much rear brake, and neither can street riders.

LATE BRAKING? FAGETABOUTIT!! Aggressive braking has no place on the street, except in emergencies. Even in racing, aggressive last-second braking is done for position change only. In other words, racers use extreme late braking to move them past an opponent at the entrance of a corner, effectively blocking the opponent's line. This type of braking will actually result in a slower lap time, because the bike is often inside the ideal racing line and probably a bit out of shape, ruining mid-corner speed and the all-important drive off the corner.

Left: Fitting a small caliper reduces the rear brake's strength. Other methods to mechanically avoid lock-ups include machining holes in the rotor, cutting away brake pad and limiting brake rod movement. You don't want too much rear brake. (John Flory)

Right: The beauty of a longer wheelbase bike is its less drastic weight transfer, meaning that this Hyabusa's rear tire stays more firmly planted under hard braking than a short wheelbase, lightweight 600's would under the same conditions. Take the time to learn how much rear brake stopping power is available on your bike. (Jeff Allen)

CHAPTER 7

ALL ABOUT ENVIRONMENT

A RIDER'S ENVIRONMENT IS MORE THAN JUST WEATHER OR TRAFFIC

My whole outlook on motorcycles, motorcycle riding and rider improvement revolves around a bit of discussion and plenty of hands-on experimentation. You've got to get out there and ride that thing, because seat time helps improve everything from the daily commute to the hot racetrack lap. Theorizing is great, but squeezing the front brake lever smoothly while your bike approaches an unknown corner at 80 mph becomes more than a simple mental exercise. When the pressure rises, your body must react correctly. And those correct reactions are much easier to choose when you know and understand your environment.

Your riding environment might be a racetrack, a busy commute, a Sunday-morning canyon blast or a tour through the Rockies. If you're lucky, you ride all of the above, and I'm planning to show you that my perception of better riding actually applies to each of the riding scenarios listed. You might tour on a Gold Wing, vintage-race a TZ350 or commute 50 miles a week on an EX500, but understanding and adapting to your environment will allow you to fully enjoy whatever aspect of this sport you love.

BE ENVIRONMENTALLY FRIENDLY

The best rides begin long before your bike rolls out of the garage or exits the motel parking lot. Just like a golfer who makes a putt in his mind a dozen times before actually stroking the ball, you should plan and imagine the next ride well before slipping on a riding jacket and helmet. Street rid-

ing will always throw a few surprises at you, but many of those unexpected events can be downplayed when you have mentally previewed a ride and imagined the environment surrounding it. A rider's environment is often more complex than mere physical surroundings; it includes trees, guardrails, cars, other riders and asphalt. When you add up all the factors that affect a motorcycle ride, the word *environment* looms as large as the state of Montana.

VISUALIZE BEFORE YOU RIDE

In my job as an instructor at the Freddie Spencer High Performance Riding School, I met the students at the hotel and shuttled them to the Las Vegas Motor Speedway in a big Ford van. For 40 minutes each school day, I had direct responsibility for the well-being of the students. I began each morning by listening to the Las Vegas traffic report, previewing the drive, playing out in my mind the trouble areas, the places where traffic habitually slows, the spots where lane closures confuse out-of-state drivers, the sections where idiots dive from the left lane to the exit ramp

Left: Failing to recognize the subtleties of your environment could be costly. This is true whether you're racing a vintage bike on narrow tires in the rain against strong competition on a racetrack lined by walls and crisscrossed with paint lines, or riding on canyon roads that are dusted with sand and dirt. (Courtesy of *Cycle World*)

Right: Riding on the opposite (left) side of the road in countries like England, Australia or Japan presents a special challenge to U.S.-trained riders, but a little planning and visualization goes a long way toward avoiding mistakes. Take the time to sketch intersections and your path through them, mentally staying left of oncoming traffic. Finally, draw an arrow pointing left on your tachometer as a constant reminder.

without a signal. Before I loaded the van, my mind ran through all the known problems and imagined a few of the unknowns. And this was just for a van drive!

Getting your brain started early works for the daily commute, the Sunday race or the Saturday morning canyon romp. In fact, it takes more environmental management to ride well on the street than to ride well on the track, and I'll venture to say that the best street riders have as many decisions to make per second as do the best roadracers.

In this chapter I'll do something I've been told can't be done: teach judgment. Too often, experienced riders have gained good judgment only through painful mistakes, but I hope this chapter will help to make the learning curve shorter and less difficult for novices and experts alike.

CHECK YOUR SPEED

Where are you going and what's the schedule? I made myself a promise to speed only if I was late for a significant event or having a great time. You might want to adopt this approach, because getting an expensive ticket while cruising at 80 mph down a boring freeway is pretty stupid. Many of us simply ride fast all the time, no matter what. That's a bad habit, not simply because of tickets, but also because of safety. It doesn't take many tickets to ruin your driving record, your insurance and, ultimately, your driving privileges. And too much speed makes it extremely difficult to avoid accidents, due to the fact that it takes longer to stop a

bike from 70 mph than 50 mph. Save speeding for making meetings with the company president or for enjoying your favorite canyon road, river run or back-country twisty.

MOISTURE

Weather is an important factor in every ride because it affects traction and vision. When you are properly prepared, riding in the rain is a gas, but it's no time for heroics. The only time to ride fast in the rain is if money and points are on the line. For me, that meant Sunday afternoons at an AMA national. Period. Rain riding is a traction crapshoot, and luck and chance play as big a part in high-performance rain riding as do skill and planning. Yes, it helps to be extremely smooth in the wet stuff, but street riders don't have sticky rain tires or a controlled racetrack environment.

Above right: Your neighborhood just might be the most dangerous place to ride, studies show. Often when drivers and riders get near home, they allow the familiarity of their surroundings to reduce their awareness. As a motorcyclist you need to draw an imaginary circle around any location you leave on cold tires, whether it's the local hangout or your garage, and ride conservatively until the tires have warmed. (Brian Blades)

Below right: Traction control and anti-lock brakes aren't included on this Yamaha R7 Superbike, leaving pilot Anthony Gobert in charge of monitoring traction front and rear in this wet race. Successful rain racers are relaxed and smooth, just like successful dry-weather racers. (Brian J. Nelson)

Below: Yeah, that's snow. But we were all ready for it because we checked the forecast and brought rain gear and electric vests. Despite riding sport bikes capable of 170 mph, we just safely putted through the cold dampness. (Jeff Allen)

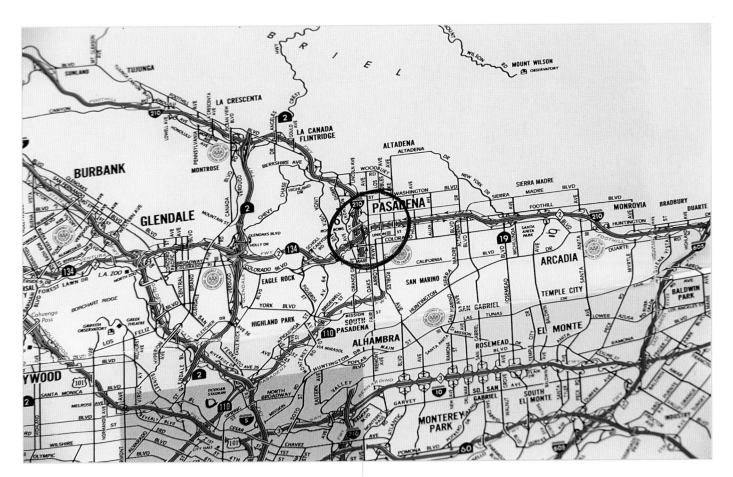

You should go slow, lean over timidly, work the controls smoothly, wear bright clothing, avoid riding over painted lines and simply refuse to take chances. Enjoy the wet weather, but don't challenge it.

Former *Motorcyclist* magazine editor Art Friedman once told me about his ill-fated experiment to judge braking traction in the wet: "I wanted to see how hard I could stop," he said, "so I just kept stopping harder and harder. I finally locked the front brake and fell down!" We all know that different pavement offers different degrees of traction, but in the wet it's difficult to discern the traction level of the pavement beneath the water—so when it changes from pretty good to pretty slippery, you're down before you can adjust.

Does that mean you should practice braking in the wet? No. Practice braking in the dry, and pay special attention to *squeezing* the front brake lever initially and concentrating on your finger pressure at the lever. Remember the rules about 100 points of traction, and build toward those 100 points slowly when you're riding in the rain: *Squeeze* the brakes and *roll* the throttle on and off. No grabbing. Friedman's painful experiment shows us that even an extremely good street rider has trouble judging wet-weather traction.

Finally, slow down when it's raining. Take no chances. Survive, because the sun will shine again.

COLD TIRES MEAN LOW GRIP

Cold temperatures make rubber hard, and hard rubber doesn't offer much traction. Imagine leaving your garage at 8 a.m. and accelerating through the gears until you're running 65 mph down your neighborhood street. Suddenly, from behind a parked van, a station wagon backs into your path, and an approaching car fills the other side of the street. Too bad that front tire's cold, because cold tires don't stick well and you need to stop now. A warm front tire would haul you down with no problem, but that hard piece of plastic rotating around your front brake caliper just isn't ready to grip. You either fall down and slide into the station wagon or hit it

while upright. Either way sucks. The lesson is that if you fail to account for part of your environment (in this instance, a cold front tire), you pay a big price for that lack of judgment. (For the purposes of this example, we'll forget the fact that you were riding 40 mph over the speed limit...more bad judgment.)

Tires warm through use, and it isn't just racers who need warm tires to survive. On a hot summer day, your tires will reach working temperature in a very short time due to the ambient air temperature and hot pavement. But on a chilly spring morning, it might take several miles of riding to heat the tires to the point where they work well under demanding conditions. Think about tire temperatures every time you fire your bike, and if they're cold, keep your speed low. As you refine your feel at the handgrips, you'll begin to notice how uncomfortable the bike feels on cold tires, as if something just isn't right. It isn't. Riding slowly on cold tires makes sense for the World Superbike champion or the everyday commuter.

THE BIKE

Your bike's characteristics are a significant part of your environment, and it pays to realize what your machine can and can't do. If you try to follow a 600cc sport bike into a downhill, decreasing radius corner on your 10-year-old cruiser, you stand a good chance of dragging foot pegs and other parts on the ground long before the other bike is near its cornering limits. Likewise, if your buddy on her 600 tries to accelerate into heavy traffic at 2500 rpm, her engine may not be making enough power to accelerate hard. Both scenarios are potentially dangerous if the rider fails to realize the weak points of his motorcycle, yet the danger is easily avoided in each case. Know your bike and respect its limitations.

Interestingly enough, a motorcycle's real or perceived shortcomings often change with time and experience. A perfect example comes to mind from 1992, when I spent a week testing all the open-class sport bikes with *Motorcyclist*. After five days of seat time on the latest, greatest bikes available, on Sunday morning I pulled my 1983 Suzuki Katana 1100 out of the garage, plunked a passenger on the back and headed out with five friends for a day of fun. My trip almost ended early when I exited the freeway and turned the bike aggressively into a left-hand corner leading to our favorite canyon. My brain was accustomed to 1992-style lean angle from riding the new bikes all week, but my butt was on a fully loaded 1983 motorcycle. I ran out of cornering clearance, the centerstand and sidestand hit the pavement and the bike slid sideways toward the gutter and curb. For some reason, the tires regained traction, and the Katana righted itself. The old Kat could be hustled through corners relatively quickly, but not with two people aboard, and not with abrupt steering inputs. Fortunately, I was given a second chance to appraise my riding environment.

TIRE CHANGES

Keep tire details foremost in your mind. As your tires wear, your riding must be adjusted accordingly, because an old, worn tire will not only stick poorly but will steer poorly as well. Since you ride on new tires only a small percentage of the time—they don't stay new forever—tire wear is something you must constantly monitor and respect. I cringe when I hear street riders blame a crash on worn tires, because the tires did not wear out during the pre-crash ride. They were worn before the ride started, and the rider should have either changed them or adjusted his riding accordingly. Let's look at ways you can adjust the way you ride to account for worn tires.

THE TIRE ENVIRONMENT:
100 POINTS OF TRACTION ON A SLIDING SCALE

The environmental issues discussed in this chapter have a huge effect on the 100 points allotted to each tire. Although environmental factors cannot actually take away points from either tire, they can adjust the scale on which those 100 points are based. Here's an example: A hot, new, sticky front racing slick has 100 points of total traction, and the scale is very high at the start of the race. Forty laps later, that slick still has 100 points of total traction available, but due to wear and heat, the scale is now considerably lower. Suddenly the skies open and rain slashes down. Has the tire lost traction points? No, there are still 100 points of available traction to be split between braking, accelerating and cornering, but the wet pavement and grooveless tire mean that the scale of those traction points is very low. The rider can still use the brakes, can still corner and can still blend the two, but a finer touch is needed because the rain has lowered the overall traction scale considerably. Practically speaking, this means not braking as hard and not carrying as much lean angle. Keep in mind that the tire will stop and steer with the same characteristics as it did in the dry, but will reach its finite traction limits much earlier. Consequently, the importance of adding braking, accel-

erating and steering points in a smooth and controlled manner becomes paramount. If your right hand moves abruptly in a reduced-traction environment, no tire technology will save you.

You can apply this same thinking to tire compounds. A touring tire designed to last 20,000 miles has a lower traction scale than a DOT-legal roadracing tire and won't respond as well to aggressive control inputs, trail-braking or accelerating hard while leaned over. All those things are possible, but they simply can not be done at the same level as they can on a sticky sport tire.

Tire wear clearly affects traction points. Unfortunately, it isn't always obvious to riders—even racers—who continue to use the side of the tire for aggressive braking or accelerating rather than reacting to tire wear by standing the bike up more before accelerating, and braking more upright during the corner entrance. Watch your favorite championship-winning roadracer on video and see how he takes away lean angle slightly before truly accelerating off a corner late in the race. Watch how he slows the bike in a straight line a bit longer late in the race rather than risk deep trail-braking on a beat-up tire. Champions realize that a tire's traction scale slowly slides downward, and they adjust braking, accelerating and lean angle points accordingly.

Tires wear in several different ways. The first is obvious upon visual inspection because the tread is thinner. Hard-core sport bike riders wear out their tires on the sides, while most others wear out their tires in the center. Standing above the tire looking down at the profile, you can

The environment of thieves: Bike shows, races, rally weekends, anywhere bikes are parked. Protect your bike by taking steps to lock, alarm or disable it. Deny thieves your bike by being prepared. (John Flory)

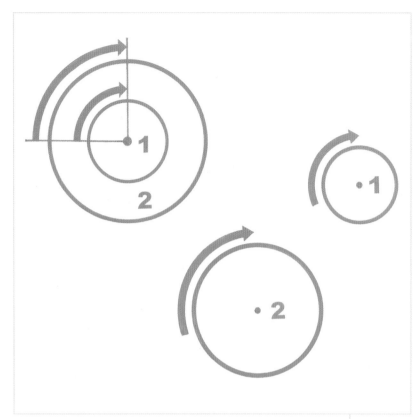

see the changes in the tire's radius. Closer inspection shows worn rubber and the tread-wear indicators (small rubber blocks at the bottom of the tread grooves). When the main tread is worn flush to the tread-wear indicators, it's time to think about a new tire.

Heat cycles—the number of times a tire has gone from cold to hot—have a great deal to do with traction levels, as much as or more than simple tread depth. How many times has that tire been heated and cooled? For racers, that question is more important than tread depth because every heat cycle cooks some stickiness out of the tire.

Before every ride, and especially every sport ride, check your tires and understand that if they're significantly worn, their traction scale is reduced. This means braking and accelerating must not only be smoother, but more lightly applied and at less lean angle. Keep that in mind as you hook up with your friends at the gas station, and know that if the pace gets turned up, your tires' performance limits are lower than they were a week ago.

THE HUMAN ENVIRONMENT

The human environment must be addressed, adjusted and managed just like the weather and tires. The right partners can make a ride perfect; the wrong ones can ruin it. If you ride with idiots, their idiocy will eventually affect you. That's a promise. This can mean something as mild as a speeding ticket, but it also can mean helping them out of a ditch or getting rear-ended as you enter a hairpin corner.

In 1988 I bought a car in Florida and drove it home to California. My trip involved back roads, and midway through Texas I came around a corner and arrived on the scene of what looked like a bomb blast. Motorcycle parts were scattered across the road, and two bodies lay motionless near a BMW sport-touring bike. The accident had just occurred, and I rushed to render first aid, helped by several other motorcyclists from the injured riders' group.

In the first five minutes, we had the two injured riders, a husband and wife I'll refer to as Tom and Linda, lying on their backs with their right legs elevated in an attempt to stop the bleeding from their almost-severed lower legs. With their legs elevated, we took turns squeezing the pressure points on the inside of the thigh to stem the blood while we waited for the ambulance. Tom and Linda remained conscious, and as we attempted to ease the catastrophe, I pieced together the cause of the accident.

The group often rode in the Texas hill country. In the past, one of the members had proven to be a poor follower, always wanting to lead the group and riding too closely to others when he wasn't. Several of the club's members had spoken to him, but their words had little effect. He still rode with too much aggression, without enough following distance and with poor judgment of how a group works together.

On this particular day, Tom and Linda were leading the group when Tom spotted a left turn he had been looking for. He saw it a bit late, and as he thumbed his turn signal switch, he applied his brakes forcefully while maintaining his position in the left wheeltrack of the lane. Unfortunately, Mr. Aggressive was right on Tom's rear tire and not staggered to the right as he should have been. He wasn't paying attention, and when Tom decelerated, his bike clipped Tom and Linda just above the right ankle. Just after that, I arrived on the scene.

I spoke with Tom and Linda several times over the following six months as they grew accustomed to their prosthetics. Both impressed me with their positive attitudes, and their recoveries were hastened by their superb physical condition. Although Tom had served in Vietnam, Linda had nothing to prepare her for the violence of that Texas day. Her motorcycling experience had been wonderfully fun until that summer afternoon.

The lesson here is simple: Quit riding with the wrong people—the riders who can't stay to the right of the yellow line, the riders who run horrendous straightaway speeds, the riders who can't or won't be cohesive mem-

bers of the group. They will hurt you badly. Practice these words: "You ride dangerously and aren't welcome in this group," or "You make too many riding mistakes, and one of them is going to hurt someone else. We don't want you riding with our group," or "We have a riding group with certain rules that you don't adhere to. You aren't included in this group." If you're invited to ride with a group that contains members with questionable judgment, try "No thanks, I'd rather ride alone." It's imperative that you find the words to control and mold the human side of the riding environment before it hurts you. Motorcycles aren't necessarily dangerous, but some riders are.

THE ENVIRONMENT OF CORNERS: FINDING THE GOOD LINE

What is this mystical line? And what makes it good? How do you know when you're on a bad line? Who drew the line? Fortunately, I have a few answers to demystify this shadowy subject, and all street riders will benefit from understanding the basics and details of choosing a good line through a corner or combination of corners. Bad lines create bad things—you will crash, cross the centerline or ride onto the

shoulder of the road. Although bad lines become apparent immediately, riders tend to repeat the mistakes that create them. That's because running bad lines is easy, and running good lines is initially difficult.

I will avoid the term "right line" because this is not math; you can't simply add up numbers and derive the same answer as the student next to you. The good line for a fully laden touring bike will differ significantly from a line that works well for a wieldy 600 sport bike. Lean angle, corner radius, speed, cornering clearance, road surface, traffic and traction must all be figured into the mix, plus the most important ingredient—the rider's ability.

RADIUS EQUALS MPH, MPH EQUALS RADIUS AND RADIUS EQUALS SAFETY

Don't be confused by the equation above. It's quite simple. The wider the radius of a corner, the faster you can ride through it at a given lean angle, or the less lean angle you need at a given speed.

Imagine you're looking at two circles side by side on a flat, sticky skidpad from overhead. Circle one has a circumference of 40 feet and circle two has a circumference of 80 feet. Which of the two could you ride a motorcycle around faster at a given lean angle? Circle two, because it allows the motorcycle to travel faster at a given lean angle. If we borrow the term *radius* and apply it to a portion of each circle as if it were a corner, we can surmise that radius equals mph. A wider radius allows a motorcycle to go faster at a given lean angle, assuming all other factors such as traction and camber are the same.

Now, what if you were riding around circle one and wanted to begin riding around circle two? What two things could you do to adjust the radius? You could use less lean angle at the same speed, or you could increase speed at the same lean angle. Increasing your speed will increase your radius (maintaining the same lean angle of circle one), or decreasing your lean angle will increase your radius, a move that adds a large margin of safety to your riding. Less lean angle means less tire loading, so fewer cornering points are

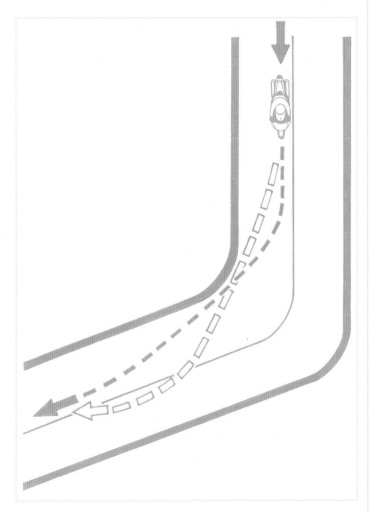

Above left: The equation Radius Equals Miles per Hour (R=MPH) refers to circles, and you can see that a rider could ride around circle two faster than circle one, simply because the radius is bigger. When you rush into corners and enter low, toward the inside of the corner, you're incorrectly tightening the radius with your lack of discipline. Increasing the radius of a corner adds safety: A bike riding around circle two will need less lean angle than a bike riding around circle one at the same speed. Increasing your radius also allows you to go faster. Racers open up radiuses for speed, street riders for safety. (Hector Cademartori)

Left: Hey, we're all human. When you get scared approaching a corner you have a tendency to turn or fade into the corner early (shown by the white dotted line). Unfortunately, that fade ruins the corner's radius when compared with a disciplined, wide approach (the black dotted line), and it also makes it difficult to see through the corner. If you fade and fail to control your speed, the bike's momentum and low entrance angle will throw it wide at the exit, and that can be fatal. (Hector Cademartori)

fled. By taking a wider entrance line, you will be effectively enlarging the radius of the corner, thus reducing the lean angle needed at a certain speed, or increasing the speed possible at a certain lean angle. This wide entrance line is the closest you'll come to a free lunch, and it's available to us all. It takes patience and discipline not to rush corners, but the payoff is safety and controlled speed.

You might know a rider who never falls down, yet rides quickly on the street. One of this rider's secrets will be running a wide, disciplined entrance line, opening the radius of every corner as far as possible given the constraints imposed by the street. Those constraints include the yellow line on the left and the white line or dirt on the right. You must respect those limits. In fact, if you ride with anyone who rides on or crosses the yellow line (except to pass), encourage them to give that centerline a wide berth. If they don't improve, quit riding with them.

Your entrance restraints also include bumps, debris and oncoming traffic. If you're approaching a right-hand corner on your favorite road and are braking and downshifting near the yellow line, be ready to move to the right quickly if a car approaches. Don't insist on running your wide entrance line. If you do, you're putting too much trust in another driver you know nothing about—he may be drunk, delirious, mean, or just stupid. Since those descriptions cover all too many of America's untrained drivers, give that car lots of room.

required, which means more braking and accelerating points are available. The reason a rider would try to open the radius of any corner is that less lean angle is always safer and feels more comfortable.

Lean angle means comfort. If a rider is forced to lean over farther than he ever has, it's extremely uncomfortable, even scary. Many riders, when surprised with a tightening corner, will stand the bike up and ride off the road, rather than continue to lean the bike into the decreasing radius corner. Physically, the bike may be capable of making the corner, but the rider's brain just isn't ready for another three or four degrees of lean angle. That's the beauty of enlarging the radius of a corner—you can ride through that corner faster, but at the lean angle you are comfortable with.

MAKING A GRAND ENTRANCE

The initial difficulty in setting up a turn begins at the corner entrance. Many riders rush the entrance, carrying too much speed into the corner, forcing themselves to stay on the brakes too hard and too long before trying to turn the bike. This is frightening, and when you get scared, you turn into the corner too early because there's plenty of comforting pavement there. This low, tight corner entrance simply makes the corner's radius tighter, which adds to the problems faced by the rider rushing the entrance. Remember, if the radius is tighter, you should either lean over more or slow down more. The first option is dangerous, and the second option isn't always easy to do.

A corner's maximum radius can be enjoyed only if the rider has the discipline to run a wide entrance line deeper into the corner. All the effort you've spent rolling off the throttle, squeezing on the brakes and smoothly downshifting will help this disciplined, controlled corner entrance because the bike will remain settled and your brain unruf-

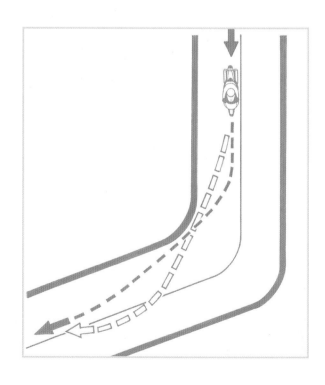

WIDE ENTRANCE: GREAT BRAKES, GOOD TURN-IN

The wide entrance line allows the rider to see farther into the corner before committing to the corner. Since the bike is upright longer, any visual surprises can be dealt with by simply braking harder or farther into the corner. In the canyons of California, you're often peering around a cliff, rock, or tree hiding the exit of the corner, so running a wide entrance line offers a better view before the bike has to be leaned over. Because riders deal with a dynamic environment that includes police, cars, gravel, kids, animals and myriad other obstacles that appear unannounced, the eyes become the primary warning device. A wide entrance line gives your primary warning device a better chance to function.

But—and there's almost always a but—this classic wide entrance line requires the perfection of your steering skills. If you plan to run your bike farther into the corner, you'll be forced to turn in less time and less distance than you would had you turned into the corner early. When you turn early, you can't turn as quickly because you'll run off the inside of the corner. On the other hand, if you turn late, you also must turn efficiently or you'll miss the corner. Your ability to turn the bike will help dictate your corner-entrance point, as will your bike's tires, steering geometry, wheelbase and weight.

Notice the word I use to describe a good turn: efficient. Not quick, flick, hammer, throw...those words denote aggression and have been part of riders' vocabularies for too long. You're going to *squeeze* the brakes and smoothly *roll* on the throttle, so carry those methods to adding lean angle points as well. Yes, certain corners require quicker steering, but keep efficiency in mind and don't simply throw your bike into a corner—trying to steer your bike

quickly will not work in all corners. For those who flick their bikes into every corner, modern tires will probably stick 999 out of a 1000 times, but that one slip will be a doozy. Do not grab the brakes, yank on the throttle or throw the bike into the corner, because you want to add and remove traction points in a controlled manner. You can add traction points quickly, but not suddenly. There's a big difference.

ENTRANCE TO APEX AND BEYOND

An apex is simply the point where you get closest to the right edge of your lane in a right-hand corner, or to the left edge (yellow line) in a left-hand corner. In a corner, a good line will almost always feature a "late" apex, meaning that the bike comes closest to the edge of the lane farther around the corner. What happens at or near the apex of the corner becomes vitally important for safety and rider longevity, so let's discuss this in more detail.

EARLY APEX

If you find yourself adding lean angle after the apex just to stay in your lane, you have turned too early. A bike should be at maximum lean angle at or just before the apex of a corner, and it's at this apex that the drive off the corner should be underway. In other words, you should be standing your bike up off the corner at or just past the apex, putting the meat of the rear tire to work. At the apex, the tire is giving the majority of its 100 rear tire points to cornering traction, so the bike must be stood up as the power is rolled on. The rider who apexes early and adds lean angle after the apex just to stay in his lane will find a world of trouble if he also tries to accelerate off the apex. Remember that the rear tire

Above left: Your environment is the right lane. Running straight through a section like this is a crime—both literally and metaphorically—and it's a sure sign you aren't in control of your bike's speed and direction. That can be a fatal mistake. (Brian Blades)
Below left: Please look at this same corner (shown on page 77) again so I can emphasize how important it is to get your bike turned efficiently when running a wide entrance. Practice steering your bike from upright to the necessary lean angle in one smooth movement, using the techniques addressed in chapter 4. And remember: Look where you want to go. (Hector Cademartori)
Right: How do you find a good apex? The white dotted line illustrates an early apex and the resulting exit line that could throw the bike into the oncoming lane. Anytime you're approaching the edge of your lane or the edge of the track at an abrupt angle on the exit, you either apexed too early or missed the apex (ran wide) by a considerable margin. The thin black line shows the exact opposite of the white dash—turning too late. The rider on the thin black line went into the corner too far and turned too late, exiting the corner on the right side of the lane. The problem here is that the thin-black-line rider thinks this is a very sharp corner and must slow way down to negotiate it. On the track, the rider of this overly late-apex line risks being centerpunched by anyone on the correct (thick black) line because the speed differential at the apex will be huge. You know the thin black line doesn't work because the exit line doesn't take advantage of the available lane. Finally, the thick black line works, correctly splitting the difference and arriving at the apex with the bike pointed down the next straight. At the apex, the rider of this line can make a decision about how the bike exits the corner, based on applying the throttle, not on controlling the bike's momentum. (Hector Cademartori)

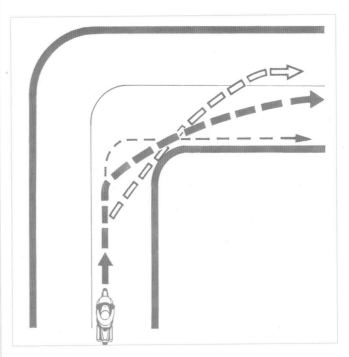

has a finite amount of traction available, and combining lean angle and acceleration points at the same time are the first steps to a hospital visit.

A nice wide, controlled entrance makes a good apex possible. If you get the bike out of shape entering the corner, it's easy to miss the apex, or run wide of the apex, by a few feet or more because your lack of control delayed the turning of the bike. Missing the apex by a few feet effectively makes the road more narrow, reducing the amount of radius and pavement you can take advantage of. As you have learned, that means you must go more slowly or lean over more just to make a given corner.

Since the apex of a corner generally represents the point of maximum lean angle, it becomes a reference point to help determine when to begin the drive off the corner. There might be corners where you brake right past the apex because a tighter corner follows immediately, but getting the apex will give you the ability to select the necessary control for the upcoming future. At the apex of a corner, you should be able to see the exit of the corner, and your eyes should find the point of maximum exit radius. That will be near the white line or road edge in a left-hander, and near the yellow line in a right-hand corner (providing there's no oncoming traffic) or, finally, the best entrance to the next corner. Missing the apex by a few inches or a few yards removes a confidence-inspiring reference point and will delay acceleration. That's because when a bike runs wide, it often takes more lean angle to make the corner, meaning that acceleration is impossible. Nail that apex, however, and it will become simple to pick the bike up and accelerate away. I can't stress enough how important it is to get your bike down to the apex of a corner. It's safer, it's faster...and what more is there?

OVERLY LATE APEX

Let's go to the other extreme and discuss apexes that are reached too late. You can define this late apex by looking at

the angle at which the rider reaches the yellow or white line at the corner exit, if he reaches it at all. You've seen how an early apex throws the bike at the yellow or white line at a very steep angle, requiring the rider to lean over just to stay in the lane. In contrast, a rider making a late apex will never reach the yellow or white line at the exit because his turn-in was so late that the bike's momentum simply carries it off the corner on a low exit line. The problem with the overly late apex is that the rider makes every corner much tighter than it really is, forcing him to either go more slowly than necessary or to lean over farther than necessary. And as an important side note, the rider who makes overly late apexes is also one of the most dangerous people on a track. His corner entrances are significantly slower and his turn-in so sharp that he blocks passing riders with surprisingly low speeds at the apex.

DOUBLE-APEX CORNERS

Some corners feature two apexes. These are bends of approximately 180-degrees—corners that come back upon themselves. It's easy to get lazy at the entrance to these corners, but the first apex is vital because it gets the bike

Left: Get your apex right so you can use all the pavement at the exit. This rider's tight apex allows him the total width of the racetrack. He can increase throttle points as he takes away lean angle points. For street riders in a narrow lane, using the available pavement (if it's clean) is even more important. (Jeff Allen)

Above right: Look closely at the dirt along the white line and you will see why these riders aren't using the entire width of the lane at the entrance. Welcome to the real world, where you can be forced into a "low" entrance by gravel, bumps, holes and dead squirrels. Don't insist on picture-perfect lines when traction is threatened. (Jeff Allen)

Right: Double-apex corners demand that you not be lazy at the entrance. Get the bike properly turned into the first half of the corner, because then you have options and a chance to deal with unexpected problems. Riders who simply roll into the first part of a double-apex corner often find themselves running wide mid-corner with a tremendous amount of lean angle. Think of point B (the turn-in point for the second part of the corner) as the most important point in this corner, and B is easier to get to when you nail that first apex. (Hector Cademartori)

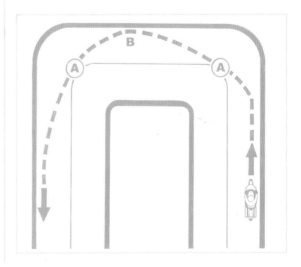

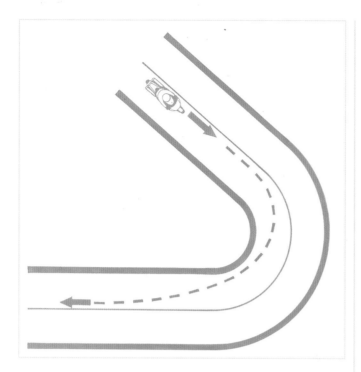

DANGEROUS DECREASING-RADIUS CORNERS

We've all experienced the fright of entering an unknown corner only to find it becoming tighter midway through. These decreasing-radius corners require a wide entrance line, which allows the rider to see farther into the corner and stay upright longer before adding lean angle. Decreasing-radius corners are hell for riders who don't trail-brake (see chapter 6) because of our simple equation: Radius equals mph. A rider who can trail-brake simply stays on the brakes into the corner, reducing the bike's speed and thus tightening the bike's turning radius. Seeing the exit before you accelerate really makes sense in a decreasing-radius corner because early acceleration would begin to widen the bike's radius just as the corner tightens. If necessary, the brakes can be used right down to the apex, a helpful technique when hustling along an unknown road.

GET THAT APEX

Uphill turns, downhill bends, wide constant sweepers—the list of potential corner combinations is long, but don't get confused by elevation changes, lines of sight or debris. Every corner has an apex, and every corner will be better if you can somehow increase its radius. Gravel, bumps and potholes might limit your line choices, but the habit of reaching your deepest lean angle at or just before the apex is a safe and smart way to ride. It's also safe and fast, but that might not matter to you. Speed is a bonus when the bike is in the right place.

For sport riders, the environment isn't just a single corner followed by a straight followed by a single corner. Our environment hooks together sweepers, kinks, hairpins and everything in between. Picking lines and apexes might sound straightforward reading it here in black and white, but as your bike rushes between corners, it becomes tempting to turn too early and abandon everything we've discussed.

Don't do it. Stick with positioning the bike for a wide entrance. Look for the apexes and judge whether your chosen apex was too early (if you needed to add more lean

pointed into the corner. If you miss that first apex, it's easy to run wide, which can be fatal in a right-hand corner with traffic coming. Make sure you recognize these double-apex corners as important to turn the bike into, not simply float into.

In a double-apex corner, the most important thing is the bike's position three-quarters of the way through the turn. It's at this point that you need to begin setting up the exit by moving the bike out wide in the lane and looking for the second apex and the corner's exit. Remember this: You can't accelerate in a double-apex corner, or any corner, until you see the exit. Sure, you can pick up the throttle to maintenance throttle, but you can not get greedy halfway through the corner and begin accelerating. This results in the bike running wide just when it should be slowing to turn down to the second apex. If you do it correctly, the bike will touch the second apex, and you can begin to stand it up off the corner by gently increasing throttle and reducing lean angle.

As the bike swooshes past the apex and you begin to stand it up on the tire to drive out of the corner, go ahead and use all the space available in your lane to widen your exit line. There's no reason to leave the bike leaned over off the corner if you can safely decrease your lean angle and take advantage of the available real estate. (Remember that the available real estate is the right lane, and the right lane only. Never cross that centerline, except to pass.) It's safer to put more tire on the ground if you can, so get used to standing the bike up on the exit if possible, within the constraints of lane width, road debris, bumps and oncoming traffic.

Above left: Decreasing-radius corners, the kind that tighten up at the exit, reward trail-braking and good use of the eyes. If you make a rule of not accelerating until you see the exit, unknown roads will become much more fun. (Hector Cademartori)

Above right: Eric Bostrom goes line to line in an effort to open the radius of every corner. More radius is more speed or less lean angle. Less lean angle is important to a Superbike rider trying to make a tire last 40 minutes. (Brian J. Nelson)

Right: This rider has failed to control the bike's entrance speed, and is now at the mercy of the bike's momentum. Unfortunately, that momentum is carrying the rider into the other lane and an oncoming car. This rider will be forced to add lean angle to stay in the right lane, but ideally you want to be decreasing—not increasing—lean angle after the apex. Exit a right-hand corner at the left edge of the lane because you have carefully increased throttle from the apex of the corner, not because you have been thrown to the left edge by momentum. (Hector Cademartori)

angle after the apex just to make the corner), or too late because you found yourself exiting the corner on the inside, without the bike wanting to stand up off the corner. Get the apex right, and the bike practically rides itself.

Hitting your apexes gives you options on the exit. Let's look at a right-hand corner. At the apex, with your eyes up to the exit, you are ready for anything. If a car is approaching with two wheels in your lane, leave the throttle shut for a low exit. If a heap of gravel is next to the white line, pick up the throttle to take away lean angle. If there's a log in the road, your bike placement allows you to take away lean angle immediately as you brake hard. With the options gained by a good entrance and nice apex, you aren't taken along for the ride. You're in control.

Unraveling a serpentine stretch of pavement, unlocking a combination of corners, remains one of the biggest thrills of riding. It takes discipline, patience and skill, plus an awareness of the ever-changing environment you're lucky enough to ride in.

LESSONS FROM THE RACETRACK

A RACER'S ENVIRONMENT Racers have a more confined environment to worry about, but they spend a huge amount of time and brain power examining road surface, weather and competing riders. And that pales in comparison to the time and thought they put into their bikes and equipment.

CHANGING TIRE CONDITIONS You can't win a race on a new tire—because by the time a race is over, no tire will still be considered new. Racers must learn to adapt to the decreasing grip of an abused tire late in the race. That means less aggressive trail-braking at the entrances to corners and

more subtle acceleration off the apex of the corner. It also means using less lean angle by hanging farther off the bike, a technique that maintains the bike's cornering radius while running less lean angle.

KNOW WHEN TO GO SLOW Poor judgment often eliminates racers early in their careers. This often boils down to over-enthusiastic use of the throttle and an ensuing high-side, or rushing corner entrances in the mistaken belief that using your brakes less is better. Getting the corner entrance right while racing is just as vital as when street riding. Freddie Spencer says, "Blow the corner entrance and nothing else matters." Kenny Roberts says, "Slow in, fast out." That's six world championships talking.

LINE TO LINE The best racers use all the track available at the entrance (far to the right entering a left-hander), then clip the apex with only millimeters to spare between their tires and the edge of the track. Finally, they exit on the far edge of the track to get the maximum available radius of the corner. The rest of us can do the same within the constraints of our lane. Crossing the yellow line on the street would be equal to a crash on the racetrack. Treat that yellow line like a cliff or wall.

"SCRUB IN" NEW TIRES It's common for a racer to start a race on a new tire, using the single warm-up lap to scrub it in. The warm-up lap on new tires might involve deep lean angles and significant brake and throttle pressures, but the racer adds those inputs in an ultra-smooth manner.

RAIN SUSPENSION Racers want to take advantage of how a motorcycle loads the front and rear tires, so when it rains, racers go significantly lighter on the suspension settings. This makes perfect sense because brake and throttle pressures won't be as high in the wet, so lighter suspension settings (spring and damping) are dialed in.

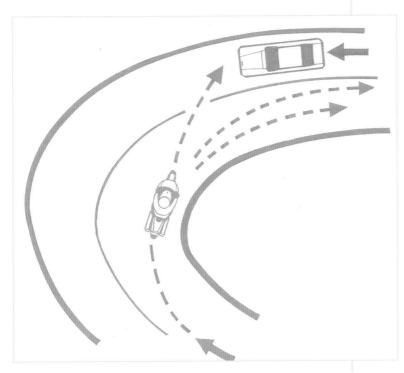

CHAPTER 8

GETTING ON TRACK

THINK OF THE RACETRACK AS A CONTROLLED ENVIRONMENT WHERE YOU CAN PRACTICE YOUR SKILLS

This is not a roadracing book, but I hope this chapter convinces you of the rewards the racetrack holds for us all. You will benefit enormously from track time even if you have no interest in actually going racing.

Why do I believe it is so important to introduce more street riders to the delights of a closed-course racetrack? The track is an environment that stresses skill and technique without the severe punishment for mistakes that the street doles out. The racetrack encourages you to focus on your skills, and as you have probably realized, skill is the only factor that consistently keeps you alive. (You can never count on luck.) Every veteran rider I know feels that time spent circling a racetrack adds a huge measure of skill in a very short period.

Track riding focuses you on the basics of motorcycle operation—accelerating, braking and cornering—and on the skills needed to perfect those basics. The environment leaves you free to experiment and expand your performance envelope, leaning over farther, accelerating harder, braking better. These skills will not only save you in an emergency,

they will also make your next ride more confident and fun. When your mind is free to focus exclusively on riding, your skill level starts to improve in quantum leaps.

RACETRACK, NOT RACING

Throwing you into the middle of a 600cc SuperStock club race would teach you nothing but panic management. This chapter is not about racing, it is about the racetrack—a closed course where all the vehicles are going the same direction and there's no surprise gravel, oncoming cars or cops to worry about. If you think the track might be too dangerous, consider that the street offers as many or more challenges. Since the track rarely changes from lap to lap (barring rain or crashes), the street rider's need to handle the unexpected is lessened. There are also flagmen at every corner waiting to announce any possible changes before you get to them. Similarly, the traction level of the track surface remains constant, allowing you to experiment with tire traction on a known surface rather than the often unknown grip of public roads. Finally, at the track you'll be surrounded by motorcycle

Left: I know, you love speed. Well, so does this guy, and he reserves this level of lean angle and speed for a racetrack. One-way traffic, no speed limits, reliable traction, no cops...heaven? Yes, and it's found only at the track. (Brian Blades)

Right: No, you don't need Kurtis Roberts' Honda RC51 Superbike to participate in a track day. Almost every modern street bike makes a fantastic track tool with surprisingly few modifications. (Brian J. Nelson)

riders intent on the same thing you are rather than the myriad vehicles you encounter on a morning commute or Saturday afternoon street ride. As unlikely as it sounds, riding on the track might be the safest mileage possible!

MY FIRST TIME, AND THEN MY FIRST TIME DOING IT RIGHT

If only I'd known what I know now the first time I took my bike to the racetrack. In 1982 I lived in Salt Lake City, Utah, and worked at State Sport Suzuki. *Rider Magazine* reported that the roadracing club in Colorado was having street races at Steamboat Springs. I prepped my Suzuki Katana 1000, and my pal George McQuiston and I went to the races. I signed up in the novice class, went out to practice in the rain and fell down while braking for a hairpin corner. George fixed the mangled bits and I did okay in the race. I was then allowed to race in the expert race, where I once again fell down in the rain. Was I in over my head? You bet.

In 1984 Art Friedman hired me at *Motorcyclist*. The magazine occasionally tested bikes at Willow Springs Raceway in California, and I had a chance to run around a racetrack with no pressure, no competition, no racing. What I learned during those testing days was invaluable and further highlighted all the things I didn't know when I went racing at Steamboat. Few riders will be lucky enough to participate

in magazine testing days, but open testing days are available at most tracks through the local roadracing club or riding school. Take advantage of them, but don't feel pressured to race.

TRACK TIME

The challenge of the racetrack is simple in concept but enormously difficult in execution. The concept: Lap as quickly as possible in a repeatable way. The execution: more complex and tricky than you can possibly imagine. And the difficulty of execution provides the immeasurable satisfaction of doing it well, which explains the addiction to the racetrack that many of us have developed. Nothing demands a balance between man and machine as much as motorcycle roadracing, and at the track, that balance constantly improves and expands, thrilling us at every step of the journey.

For many street riders, competitive urges often bubble to the surface during a group ride, and when two or more egos collide, the pace can become far too fast for the street. And when speeds escalate, rider skill often takes a back seat to pure bravado and careless risk taking. It isn't the best rider who appears fastest on the street, but the rider willing to take the most chances—until that rider crashes, which is almost always catastrophic when pushing

the limits on public roads. If you want to hone your riding skills to a level that matches your speed, then racetrack laps are the perfect solution.

Rather than bravado and bluster, lap times speak volumes about rider skill. The confidence of knowing your skill level at the track will hold your ego in check when the urge to race on the street rears its head. Once you realize what truly fast riding is—it's a type of riding available only at a racetrack—the street becomes a place to enjoy your bike, the day and your friends. Pushing the limits on the street will soon seem as intelligent as playing Russian roulette. I speak from experience, having watched acquaintances visit the racetrack for the first time and then re-evaluate their priorities on the street.

STRANGE NEW WORLD

Racetrack trepidation is easy to explain. You're going into an unknown environment, a world already occupied by riders experienced with the lingo, the routine and the layout of this strange new world. Remember that each of these more experienced riders had to begin where you are now, with that first visit to the track. They struggled through the efforts of loading bikes, filling out paperwork, setting up a pit location and finally getting onto the track, just like you are now. Even if you come across some superior attitudes, remember that Mr. Attitude went through exactly what you are experiencing. Ask questions, follow directions, give yourself time by arriving early for everything and you'll soon be a veteran track rider. If this chapter does nothing but relieve your anxiety about visiting a racetrack, I will consider it a success.

DISCOVERIES ON THE TRACK

It's no secret that most of today's sport bikes are designed with the racetrack in mind, especially when you consider the "Win on Sunday, Sell on Monday" attitude that drives the market. If a manufacturer wants to sell a bunch of sporting 600s, its first job is to make sure the bike can win races in AMA Supersport, World Supersport or at the club level. So it's safe to assume that many of the best attributes of your new sport bike can't be realized until you find yourself on a closed-course racetrack. But what will you discover there?

First, you can haul ass. While 100 mph can get pretty hairball on your favorite back road, it's fairly manageable on a 40-foot wide racetrack with no oncoming traffic. And while you may rarely use the upper reaches of your tachometer during a Sunday morning ride, you'll have a chance to become intimately familiar with redline on the track. And that's a bunch of fun, especially when you realize that big speed on the racetrack isn't half as scary as lesser speed on the street.

You'll also get a chance to become more confident with the most powerful component on your motorcycle: the front brake. Because a racetrack offers repeatable corners and uniform traction, you can sneak up on the enormous stopping ability your brakes offer. Everything about braking that's discussed in chapter 6 transfers wonderfully to the track.

Another discovery the track affords is increased use of your body as a steering device, which we covered in chapter 4. To truly realize the effect of moving your weight around

Above: Same bike, same turn, two different riders. Track riding is all about function, and the bike steers and tracks over bumps better when your center of mass (shoulder area) is placed low and to the inside of the corner, shown in the second rider's positioning. With the rider's mass lower and inside, the bike can carry more speed at a given lean angle. The top rider will find the lean-angle limits sooner, and at a lower speed than the rider below, who has committed himself to the body position suitable for track riding. (Brian Blades)

Left: Hey, ya gotta start somewhere. This photo was taken two days before my first race in 1982. I'm giving my race-prepped 1982 Suzuki Katana a shakedown ride to the local burger joint. Not visible is the wooden dowel holding the number plate on. Rob Muzzy I ain't. (George McQuiston)

approved full-face helmet, gloves, boots and a one-piece leather suit or a two-piece design that zips together at the waist. Some clubs will allow nylon street suits from Aerostich, Motoport, etc., and you'll need a good back protector. Many track riders, myself included, wear chest protectors to prevent injury to the heart and lung area. Get the best protective gear you can afford. Painful lessons have taught me to wear quality riding gear every time I ride on the racetrack, whether for magazine photo shoots, racing or just lapping for fun. I recently heard about a few riders who don't wear their back protectors during practice, reserving them for the race. How crazy is that? Wear it all—all the time.

You'll need to spend some dough on your bike as well. Don't go to the track with marginal tires, drive chain or brake pads. Have your bike freshly tuned. Bring a rear-wheel stand to ease maintenance chores, and an extra 5 to 10 gallons of fuel, which means you'll need a gas can. If your local organization requires safety wiring of all critical fasteners, you'll be buying a drill, drill bits, safety wire and safety-wire pliers, or paying a shop to do the job for you. Most organizations will require replacing your bike's coolant with straight water to avoid slippery substances on the track should you crash, so plan on buying a few gallons of distilled water and a water-pump lubricant and rust inhibitor

Above left: Dress to crash, because the money spent on good equipment will save you pain and painful medical expenses later. Think about adding hockey pants and pads under the suit, and add a chest protector to the mandatory back protector. Protection technology has accelerated the development of gloves and boots, so update those important pieces frequently. (Courtesy of *Sportbike*)

Above: Frame sliders—that black cylindrical part projecting through the fairing in this photo—protect the bike in a sliding crash, such as a low-side. Without these replaceable plastic sliders, even a second-gear spill can tear up a fully faired sport bike. Some professional tuners think that frame sliders can cause frame bending in a tumbling crash, but most decide in favor of this cheap form of insurance. (Dennis Morrison)

Right: Crashing your new open-class sport bike (this Honda CBR954 was $10,599 in 2002) hurts in many ways. Some of that pain can be diminished by investing in a less expensive track-only bike. The only bright spot in this picture is the realization that most cool project bikes begin with a crash! (Brian Blades)

the motorcycle, you need to have the freedom to experiment in a finite environment with repeatable corners and no law-men. It's a great feeling when you begin to time and coordinate your weight changes with the upcoming corners and discover just how well your bike can work.

THE DOWNSIDE

Let's talk about the downside of heading out to the track, starting with the expenses. Though it's possible to ride your bike to most lapping days, you will probably need a truck and/or trailer to get your bike trackside. The truck and/or trailer will also tote along the gas, ice chests, tools, umbrellas and other assorted items that make life nicer, including lunch and water. You will need to spend some cash on a loading ramp and tie-downs, plus some storage boxes for extra parts, tools, tape, zip-ties, etc. If your local track isn't very local, there's the cost of meals and hotels to add, as well as maintenance costs or gas money if you borrow your pal's thirsty truck.

You'll need specific equipment, starting with a DOT-

such as Redline's Water Wetter. None of this is big bucks, but it all adds up.

Resist the urge to stretch a tire's usefulness to one more track day. I can't count the thousands of dollars in wrecked bodywork produced by worn-out tires that "might have a few laps left in them." They didn't. It's important to understand that a tire's life and usability can't be measured by tread depth alone. As discussed in chapter 7, heat cycles also have a great deal to do with the level of traction available. Tires that have been through many heat cycles have lost considerable traction but may not show obvious signs of wear. I've seen tires worn to the cord in a single cycle (such as an endurance race) that will still outpace a new-looking tire that has been used for three lapping weekends over the space of six months. The latter tire looks newer, but the former tire works better. If you must stretch a tire's usefulness for one more session, remember how the 100 points of traction work, and respect the fact that the tire is less than perfect. Sneak up on its limits rather than burst over them.

Many track enthusiasts find that tires are their biggest expense because track-compound tires simply don't last as long as street-compound tires. Improved traction almost always means accelerated wear, and most riders opt for track-compound skins. Yes, street-compound tires will last longer and possibly cost less, but may not have the traction you need when the pace gets turned up on the track. I won't recommend any particular brand because I've ridden every DOT-approved track-compound tire made since 1984 and am confident that you can't find a loser in the bunch. Ask fellow riders about the tires they use and how they like them. Remember that tires often differ in their profiles, and the profile affects steering characteristics. A tire with a more triangular profile when viewed head on will steer more quickly than a broader, rounder profile. What works well on one bike may not work as well on another.

As long as we're talking expenses, you might want to hedge your bets by fitting your bike with a set of aftermarket bodywork and some frame sliders (bolt-on plastic pieces that help keep the bodywork off the pavement) in case you fall. Even just tipping over your fully faired sport bike while unloading can cost a few greenbacks, and that mistake will be less costly to fix if you have the pristine stock bodywork at home in the garage. If you want to keep spending, pack along an extra handlebar, clutch lever and brake lever and a set of grips in case you have a small spill that requires only minor surgery. You can bet that any national-level and many top club-level teams have a significant inventory of extras, so they are a possible source for at-track parts.

If you find yourself becoming hooked on track days, you

Open-class sport bikes are tremendously entertaining on the track in expert hands. But beginning riders can be so overwhelmed by a big bike's horsepower and straightaway speed that they forget about lines, trail-braking, body position, looking ahead and enjoying themselves. Bigger isn't always better, or more fun. (Brian Blades)

might consider going one step further in the expense department. Rather than risking your precious dream bike on the track, think about buying a track-ready motorcycle as your track-only bike. You probably have a good idea of what you like in a motorcycle and which bikes offer those attributes. A quick scan of the roadracing magazines/newspapers or Internet sites will overwhelm you with the variety of race bikes for sale. Think of leaving your MV Augusta F4 in the garage and picking up a clean, used Japanese 600 for $2000 to $4000. If you're not particularly mechanical, have an experienced friend or shop check out the bike for you. Typically it's cheaper to buy a well-prepped race bike than to build your own.

MISCELLANEOUS (BUT IMPORTANT) TRACK TIPS

Write big on the entry form because you'll be nervous and the small letters will look shaky.

Never miss the riders' meetings.

Learn where the officials want you to enter and exit the racetrack. Remember to always get a hand up or foot off the peg when you are preparing to exit the track.

Start drinking lots of water days before the event and stay hydrated, even on cold days.

Bring a friend to help with the bike, call him or her your Tuner and buy him or her dinner.

Go nowhere without checking your tire pressure and fuel level. That's tire pressure and fuel level every time the bike moves.

Always say a big friendly hello to those pitted next to you. You may soon need their help.

Always accept help loading and unloading, or while putting your bike on the rear-wheel stand.

If your loading ramp sucks, you will pay. Guaranteed. Get a good, wide ramp.

Hide valuables and lock up your stuff if possible. There's not much theft, but when something's missing it's usually expensive.

Bring as many chairs as possible because yours will always be in use.

Buy a sunshade/tent/canopy and stake it down the moment you erect it.

If a racer with a single-digit number speaks about the track, listen. If anyone else offers advice, thank them politely for their opinion.

Flags

Since there are no road signs or speed limits, flags are used by the corner workers or pit steward to communicate with the riders on the track. These flags are almost universally known, but each club or group will have certain rules to follow when certain flags are displayed. Learn these rules and understand that obeying them is essential to safety on the track.

Green: The practice session, qualifying session or race has started. The track is "hot"; riders are out and at speed.

Yellow, standing: Caution, control your speed, but the crash or problem is not on the racetrack. Passing is usually allowed. Often displayed one or two corner stations before the incident.

Yellow with red stripe: Caution, debris on track. Usually displayed one corner station before the incident.

Yellow, waving: Extreme caution. Crash or debris is on the pavement. No passing. Usually displayed one corner station before the incident. Watch the corner worker for hand signals that can help direct you around the problem.

Red: Cessation of practice or race due to a problem that would endanger other riders or the rescue workers. Some clubs want the racers to safely come to a complete stop, some clubs want the riders to continue back to the pits at slow speed. Usually displayed at all corner stations. Remember to raise your hand before you slow your speed, don't simply chop the throttle. That's hand up first, and then slow speed.

Checkered: Race or practice session is over. Complete the lap and return to the pits.

Black: Signals to a rider that he or she must pit immediately, due to a motorcycle problem or rule infraction. Usually displayed at the start/finish line, and often accompanied by a board with the offender's number on it. Safely exit the track and go to the hot-pit lane for instructions from the officials.

White with red, stationary: Emergency vehicle on course. Will be displayed one corner station before the vehicle.

Make a riding-gear list and check it every time, adding pieces as needed.

If you're late for the beginning of your session, don't sweat it or you'll forget something important, like that you're riding on cold tires. Take two or three laps to put some heat in them before you begin to explore the traction limits.

You'll probably forget cold tires only once, and then remember the resulting crash for the rest of your life. Get tire warmers (and a generator) if you can afford them and use them for at least 20 minutes before you ride.

Wear earplugs while riding.

Ride your own ride. As soon as you follow another rider for

Above: Each track's flag usage will be covered in the riders' meeting, but don't mistake the meaning of the checkered. It means "session over," not "stop concentrating." But some riders unplug their brains and crash on the cool-off lap. Use that lap to help your engine cool down and preserve its valves. Stay focused until you come to a stop in the paddock. (Dennis Morrison)

Left: This rider is smiling because she can load her own bike, despite being only 5'3". She learned to ride the bike up the wide ramp and into the truck by practicing first with the ramp on the ground. Pretty cool, so I married her. (Nick Ienatsch)

more than one lap, you begin to make the same mistakes and ride the same lines. Either make the pass or slow down and put some distance between yourself and the rider.

Wave to the corner workers on the cool-down lap.

Use the first lap to warm up and the last lap to cool down. Modern sport bikes run tremendous cylinder-head temperatures, and the small valves will repay you if each session is closed with a nice, low-rpm cool-down lap (not necessarily slow speed, but low rpm). But sometimes you may not get this opportunity. If you get the checkered flag near the end of the lap, I suggest you make a nice long, slow ride through the pits.

Ask a rider you respect for help with everything from lines to suspension.

Even if you're in incredible physical condition, it's a lack of mental concentration that causes most racetrack crashes. Don't ride tired.

SPECIAL SKILLS

To get the most out of a day at the track, there are several areas that require special attention, and several skills that, once mastered, will significantly improve your performance.

INTER-RIDER COMMUNICATION

While flags help the safety crew communicate with the riders, there are also ways for the riders to communicate with each other on the track. The main reason for communication is to signal to others that you are "off the pace," or simply

not riding at your best speed. Why is that important? Because your brake lights and turn signals will be either removed or taped over, and your slower speed can create huge speed differences that may not be noticeable unless you are signaling. To show others that you are off the pace, you must wave your left hand off the bar or dangle your foot off the foot peg to tell everyone, "Hey, I'm cruising here so don't expect me to rage off into this corner." For instance, if you plan to pit before the checkered flag ends the session, you must wave your arm or dangle a foot to indicate your intentions to those behind you. If you've been lapping quickly and want to cruise for a few corners, wave an arm, dangle a foot. If you're late for your session and enter the track a few laps after the session started, wave an arm and dangle a foot occasionally during that first slower warm-up lap to warn the riders who are already into their third hard lap.

Your track entrances and exits are supremely important. Make sure you know where the stewards want you to enter the track (exiting from the pits) and exit the track (entering the pits). Since you'll be entering the track on cold tires, do not dive right onto the racing line; give it plenty of room while you wait for your tires to warm up. In fact, any time you are off the pace, try to stay clear of the racing line to let other riders past without interrupting their rhythm.

The club I race with most, the Willow Springs Motorcycle

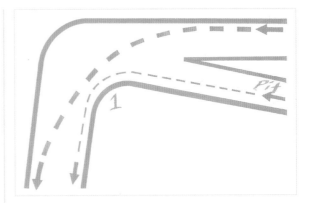

Club, will not tolerate unsafe track entrance and egress (exit). Do it wrong once and you will be spoken to by the officials. Continue unsafely and you're done for the weekend. Imagine passing a slower rider on the outside of fourth-gear turn nine, only to have that rider sit up at the exit and move across the track into pit lane! Safe entrances and exits are a big enough deal at Willow to receive constant attention from the track steward, and they are also a great habit to take anywhere you ride. Street riders need to be very aware of communicating in their environment as well. The fewer surprises America's cell-phoning drivers have to deal with, the better your chances of surviving a commute. Communication means turn signals on the street, hand signals on the track.

PASSING

You will pass and be passed by other riders at the track. Understand that it is the responsibility of the rider making the pass to do so safely. Since no one can win practice, it makes sense to pass sensibly and politely—because that's how you would like to be passed, right? For many beginning track riders, passing can be a significant challenge. They often find it's easy to catch up to another rider but then get stuck behind him for lap after lap.

Use your eyes and develop the following technique to improve your chances of making a solid, safe pass. Look past the rider you've caught, using your peripheral vision to keep tabs on her position while looking forward to find a spot on the track where you can make your move. If you and the leading rider are close in skill and speed, it may take a lap or two to discover her weak spot, or your area of advantage. But remember that you caught her by riding at your pace and your style, so don't give up on what has worked to get you this far. Stick with your lines and limits, and don't go over your head while making an unwise pass that will endanger you and the other rider.

Left: Miguel DuHamel illustrates the correct way to signal on a racetrack. While tucked in, he raises his hand before slowing the bike and sitting up to enter the pit. Riders who slow first and then put their hand up are in danger of being hit from behind. Signal first, and then slow. (Brian J. Nelson)

Above right: Unexpected moves at the racetrack have devastating consequences, and improper track entrances and exits are the most common mistakes. Riders entering the track on cold tires must learn to stay off the fast line, as illustrated here. Ugly things happen when bikes arrive in the same spot at different speeds. (Hector Cademartori)

Below: Target fixation isn't reserved for stationary targets. Resist the urge to lock your main focus onto the rider ahead, or you will simply circulate at that rider's speed. Look where you want to be—in front. (Dennis Scully)

fine for overtaking a much-slower rider, but for someone of equal speed it can get dicey.

It would be much better for the following rider to try to run a wider radius than the leading rider, carrying more speed through the corner and accelerating harder (fewer lean angle points means the use of more acceleration points), setting up the pass for the adjoining straight or next braking zone. Well-done passes begin in the preceding corner.

So what do you do if you're getting passed? Nothing, except stick with your game plan and never look over your shoulder. As a faster rider sets you up, or plans her pass, she takes into account the things you're doing on the motorcycle. If you suddenly change your methods, you become a huge unknown quantity, and the faster rider's plans have suddenly gone out the window. Also consider that more than one rider might be passing you, so a flinch or movement in reaction to the first passing rider may jeopardize the next rider, or even the one after her. Stay on your line, stay focused on your shifting, braking or steering, and simply ride as well as you can. Every time I've seen a slower rider look over their shoulder to see a faster rider closing quickly, the slower rider has bobbled and made the ensuing pass scary to witness. Keep your eyes and your focus ahead of you.

There's an adjustment you can make to stay out of trouble when riding with faster riders: Leave a bit more room at the edge of the racetrack as you exit the corners. By leaving this outside lane open, you allow the faster riders to accelerate off the corner on a wider, usually faster line. This is

There are two passes that beginning riders often misjudge with painful consequences. The first is riding around the outside of a slower rider. It's easy to misjudge the length of your motorcycle and pull over into the other rider too early, clipping his front wheel with your rear wheel. You need to give the other rider room—just because he's disappeared from your peripheral vision doesn't mean you can move over on him. In this case, as in everything related to our sport, it's better to err on the side of safety.

The second scary pass comes at corner exits, when the following rider tries to accelerate out of the corner underneath the leading rider. Think about what the following rider is asking his rear tire to do: corner on a tighter radius than the leading rider *and* out-accelerate that leading rider. Talk about a recipe for a high-side! The following rider is already carrying more lean angle points than the leader, and then tries to add more acceleration points. He's also carrying a tighter radius, which goes against the equation you learned in the last chapter: Radius equals mph. Sure, this pass is

Above: Hey, that BMW R-bike ain't no race bike! That's OK, because this guy isn't going racing. Whether race day or track day, the pit-support essentials can make or break the experience. Many one-time costs, such as a bike trailer or a canopy, will prove useful for years. Yeah, years. (I'm just trying to help you rationalize these costs...) (Brian Blades)

Right: Safe passing is a must at track days, so think about making the pass (see the circled area at the exit of turn one) when the rider is parallel to you or going away from you. In this case, the rider represented by the triangle is being passed, and the rectangle rider does it correctly by increasing the radius of turn one (remember, R=MPH) and making the pass as the triangle rider goes to the right to set up for turn two. Meanwhile, the dotted-line rider is adding lean angle in turn one, plus trying to out-accelerate the triangle rider before turn two, while the triangle rider is veering right toward the dotted-line rider. The dotted-line rider is asking his rear tire to lean over farther and accelerate harder than triangle. That's gonna get scary! (Hector Cademartori)

Above right: Experiencing consistent track days or race weekends begins at home with thorough preparation. Every unexpected mechanical event pulls your attention away from circulating the racetrack well. Don't waste time and mental energy working on your bike at the track. (Brian J. Nelson)

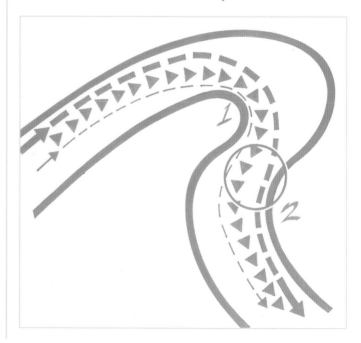

much better than staying above them as they attempt to accelerate off the corner underneath you. It's not only safer if they misjudge their exit speed or throttle application, but it will put them past you more quickly, avoiding a drag race to the next corner.

If you are passed too closely during a practice or open lapping session, resist the urge to confront the other rider. Instead, go to the pit steward or club president and ask them to speak with the rider about his passing distances and practice-session priorities. Conversely, if you find a rider limping around the track so slowly he becomes a safety hazard, ask the steward to put that rider in a slower practice group, or move up one yourself.

GREAT EXPECTATIONS

Let's walk through a typical track day and discuss what you can expect. Plan on arriving early, around 7:30 a.m., with the first session beginning at 9 a.m. You may be directed to a pit spot, but you are usually free to find your own. I like to pit fairly close to the pit exit/track entrance because there's lots of activity and you can stay in your comfortable pits until your session actually enters the track. You should think about registering even before unloading your bike, because there could be a line and you might need to fill out several forms. Many clubs and groups allow pre-registration through the Internet. Take your wallet, checkbook and health insurance information to sign-up.
Be friendly.

If it's your first time, don't be afraid to ask to speak with the pit steward, club president or head honcho. That person is making money from your presence and will be glad to walk you through the procedures, whether you're participating in a school, entering a race or just lapping the track. And hopefully while you're mucking about with sign-up, your "Tuner" will have already unloaded your bike!

Take a page from my Tuner's notebook and have your bike ready to run before it leaves your home. That means tire pressures have been checked, fuel is in the tank, lights have been removed or taped, the license plate and side-stand/centerstand removed and any other items your organization requires. If you're not sure, call ahead and get a list of necessary modifications. You then arrive at the track, unload your bike and roll it through tech inspection. Working on your bike at the track seems to increase the stress level exponentially, and there's already enough stress at the track. You may need to bring your helmet and leathers to tech as well, but get your bike through tech inspection before you start worrying about tents, chairs, carpets or umbrella girls. You want your bike sitting in line full of gas, ready and waiting.

At this point, listen to the announcements for a riders' meeting and be sure to attend. The riders' meeting is a chance for the organization to outline critical information, such as track problems, what to do in case of a red flag, how to safely enter and exit the track and any other business that needs to be brought to the riders' attention. It should also address the order of the groups, the school information and any questions that are asked. If you're

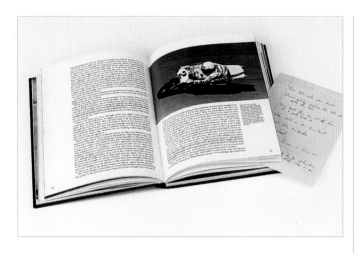

unsure of anything, now is the time to ask.

By this time, you should be sipping water, studying a track map and getting ready to ride. Each group should get a first, second, and third or final call, which gives you time to get your gear on and warm up the bike. It's easy to get ready too early, but that always beats getting ready too late. If it's hot, leave your helmet off and leathers unzipped until the final call, and remember that the final call can be delayed for quite a while if the group before you suffers a problem. It's easy to get all psyched up on the second call, put on all your stuff, start your bike and go sit in line only to find yourself in the same spot 10 minutes later. You'll get ample time on the track during the day, so it's silly to worry about being one minute late for the start of your session.

Don't accept any offers to be led around the track during the first session at a new track, unless it's a series of mandatory sighting or warm-up laps. Why? Following an experienced rider around an unknown track will only serve to scare you and lead to a tunnel-vision perspective that retards your learning curve. Instead, at the beginning of your first session, spend time learning the track layout, and always take one or two laps to heat your tires, oil, brake pads and brain at the beginning of every session. If you get out in the session late, be careful of faster traffic when you enter the track, and never enter the racing line on cold tires. Try and use the first few laps of each session to make the track your own, familiarizing yourself with things other than the color of the pavement. Look around at the flag stands and take note of passing zones and alternate lines that are available. If you enter the track and immediately go into race mode, you may always feel a bit alienated due to the fact that your surroundings never became familiar. Ride the first two or three laps of every session as if you've fitted your mental camera with a wide-angle lens rather than the zoom lens most beginning riders use. Simply put, don't try too hard on the first lap. Every racer I know has fallen due to cold tires and a hot brain, and it's a lesson with painful consequences that can easily be avoided.

TIRE WARMING

Riding on a cold tire, a new tire or a new, cold tire is exactly like riding in the rain. There is traction available, but the limits of traction are relatively low, and these limits can be easily exceeded with abrupt inputs. Now more than ever, smoothness is critical. You can *roll* your bike to its lean angle, but you can't snap it. You can *squeeze* the brakes progressively and stop quite hard, but you can't grab at the brake lever. You can go quite fast on cold tires, but never with the aggression that a hot tire permits.

A dangerous combination is a cold tire and a cold day. Cold pavement prevents the tire from coming up to its normal temperature at the usual rate, so warming your bike's tires will take even more time if the sun's not out and the air's not hot. As your riding progresses, you'll be able to feel your bike's improved comfort level as the tires "come in," or reach their operating temperatures. Before the tires warm, the bike will feel top heavy and unwieldy, as if the chassis is incorrectly set up. Don't ignore this feeling, because it's a message that things aren't right. Another lap or two, and the tires will send a message of readiness.

Don't weave to warm your tires. Most racing organizations frown on the practice due to the varying skill levels of the club racing or track day participants. Tires will heat with every revolution, so braking and cornering forces will have the tire ready in a lap or two, depending upon the speed of the rider and ambient air temperature.

LUNCH BREAK

As the day continues, you should find time between riding sessions to draw a track map and jot down some thoughts on each of the corners. Add your gear changes and draw in some cornering lines, and pay attention to the parts of the track you are unsure of. Are you downshifting once or twice? Is there a bump in that corner? Questions like these will highlight the track sections you need to focus on in the next session.

I urge you to make a map and notes for the simple reason that riding improvement begins in the mind before it's transferred to the track. To make significant progress with your riding, you must first make the improvement in your mind while sitting alone in your pits; writing down your thoughts helps you to focus on the needed improvement. If you want to jump-start your learning curve, do your thinking on paper and review your notes as often as possible, especially just before heading onto the track.

Also find time between sessions to wipe down your bike, especially the parts that will kill you if they're faulty: the brakes, chain, handlebars and levers. When you're cleaning your bike is the best time to uncover minor flaws that are on their way to becoming major problems, such as cracked brake discs, missing fasteners or a faulty master-link clip. Make sure there's a locknut on the brake lever bolt and also on the chain adjusters, and give all the bodywork a tug and a tweak. Cleanliness is the first step in safe machine preparation.

As the afternoon wears on, you'll notice a significant loss of concentration if you haven't been drinking water and eating well. You'll also notice fewer riders in your group due to fatigue, bike failures and falls. Keep this in mind when everyone is rushing about to make the first minute of the first practice; you might even want to skip the first session because you'll probably get plenty of track time later in the day.

GOALS

Having a goal for each riding session will help focus your time on the track. Those goals might include a different braking strategy, trying new overall gearing or simply trying a different body position. Broadly speaking, your goal should be improvement with every session, whether that means going faster, riding better overall or improving a particular skill. Don't feel that you should push as hard as possible in every session. Many times your best riding will come when you relax and back off on the aggressiveness, especially at the corner entrances. I've often seen students score their fastest times at the end of the day when they were simply using their final lapping session to relax and have fun.

Take advantage of your suspension's adjustability by making changes between practices. Ask an expert rider to bounce your suspension and then try a few of his recommendations. Write the changes in a notebook so you'll know where you started and how to get back to your basic settings, just in case you go the wrong way. It's fun, interesting and makes each practice a learning experience.

DONE FOR THE DAY

There's not much to say about packing up, but don't be too proud to accept help loading your bike. I've seen more bikes crashed while loading and unloading than while rid-

Right: Make a habit of tech-inspecting your bike frequently. Certain items, when loose or missing, will really hurt you: brake-caliper bolts, chain-adjusting bolts and nuts, the nut on the brake lever bolt, front-and-rear axles, brake pad retainers...I've seen crashes result from all these failures, and in every case the components had simply vibrated loose. Ultimately, that's not mechanical failure, that's human error. (Brian Blades)

Above left: It's not surprising that I found some of my own racing notes wedged inside Kenny Roberts' book, *Techniques of Motorcycle Roadracing* (co-authored by Peter Clifford). My copy of his book became dog-eared, highlighted and a frequent reference, as I hope your copy of my book will become for you. Making your own notes and drawings of corners will help improve your riding between practices. Don't waste time between sessions. (Brian Blades)

ing, so an extra set of hands is always welcome. It's a good idea to wipe down your bike again before you leave, because you often arrive home too late to care about a clean bike. Think about making a list of the needed maintenance or modifications your bike requires as you cruise home, while everything's fresh in your mind. Buy your Tuner/helper/friend/wife dinner so you can sucker them into helping you again next time. And if you did it right, there will definitely be a next time.

LESSONS FROM SCHOOL

Since this entire chapter has been about learning from the racetrack, I'll conclude by listing some of the most common mistakes instructors see at racetrack schools.

1. Trying too hard at the corner entrance. To go fast, some students feel the need to push in every section of the track. Trouble is, if you goof up the entrance, the corner is completely shot. If you get the bike out of shape going in, you are unable to choose a good line, get the bike turned,

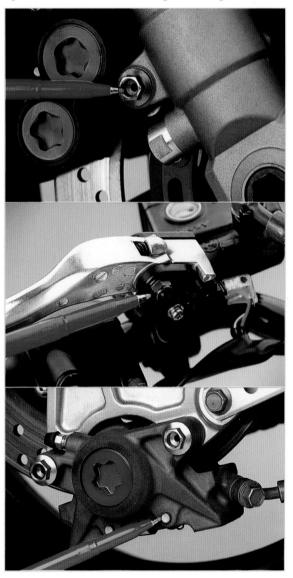

hit the apex and open the throttle early. There's an old saying: Go slower to go faster. That applies directly to students trying too hard at the corner entrance.

2. Early turn-in. This mistake goes hand-in-hand with the one above. When you scare yourself on the brakes trying to rush the entrance, you automatically let the bike drift in toward the apex because that's where all the comfortable, safe pavement is. As you drift in, you reduce the available radius of the corner. That means you must either slow down to negotiate the corner at your comfortable, known lean angle, or lean over more than you have before. That becomes uncomfortable, and some students get scared, stand the bike up and ride off the track.

3. All or nothing on the controls. I've said it before: Be smooth. The throttle and brakes aren't on/off switches, they're rheostats with an almost infinite number of settings. The best riders are adding throttle or using the brakes in minute, almost undetectable amounts. Students might initially get away with grabbing and jabbing, but as they try to go faster (and lean over farther), they will quickly overwhelm their tires' traction limits. It won't be pretty.

4. Tight shoulders and arms. Your bike talks to you in three places: the handlebars, seat and foot pegs. Of the three, the bars provide you with the most critical information about steering and traction, but you won't feel any of the communication if you've got a death grip on the handgrips. Relax those arms and shoulders and you'll find that the bike simply works better because the front end is free to respond to bumps and pavement imperfections without you rigidly holding on.

5. An immobile butt. To relax your arms, slide your butt off the seat to the inside of the corner. Ideally, the center of your butt will be on the inside edge of the seat, putting much of your weight on the inside foot peg. Place the thigh of your outside leg against the fuel tank and tighten up your stomach muscles to hold yourself in place, relaxing your arms. If you don't move off the seat far enough, you will have a difficult time relaxing your arms. To practice this, place your bike on the sidestand and hang off the left side in the manner described. See if you can let go of the handgrips. To do this, you will need to tighten your

Right: Use that body! Blatantly illegal acts on public highways are perfectly acceptable at the racetrack. And necessary. Hanging off is an important skill to master to get the most out of a modern sport bike on the track. Riders who don't hang off will be forced to run more lean angle at the same speed, and lean angle is finite. (Jay McNally)

Below: What better place to fine-tune suspension than the racetrack? The unchanging repeatability of running laps allows a consistent rider to experiment with spring preload, damping rates and ride heights. That said, here's a quote from an exceptionally good factory roadracing mechanic: "The most important suspension component to improve is the rider." (Dennis Morrison)

crotch and stomach muscles, and you'll understand why Wayne Rainey used to do 600 sit-ups a day.

6. Eyes down, surprises ahead. Students who are scared by speed and are late with the control inputs (especially the throttle) simply need to raise their horizon and look up the track. It sounds too simple, but it's amazing how frequently students make this one adjustment and open a whole new door to successful riding. Get your eyes up and feed your brain with a picture of a future you can survive.

7. Not enough brakes. As students think about riding faster, they mistakenly believe that less braking is the key. That's 100 percent wrong. The fastest riders will use their brakes more, which means earlier application, more pressure and more trail-braking, because they are carrying more speed on the straights. A 50 mph corner remains a 50 mph corner whether you're approaching at 55 mph or 120 mph. The faster rider will require significantly more braking to successfully negotiate the corner's radius because the corner won't change its radius to match your newfound speed. If you add speed, you must balance it with added braking. More speed, more brakes.

8. Not working between the corners. Let me tell you a little secret: There's a lot of work to be done between corners. Students who don't get the bike across the track to set up a wide, radius-increasing corner entrance have to either slow down or lean over farther just to make the corner. If

the exit of corner two throws the rider out to the left side of the track but corner three's entrance is far to the right, few beginning riders will work hard enough to get the bike over to the right by using handlebar pressure, knee pressure or weight change to direct the bike.

9. No off-track improvement. Most major improvements in riding come first from the brain while the body is motionless. That means studying in the pits, something that students often overlook. It's not enough to try 110 percent on the track—you must also make that effort off the bike.

10. Overemphasizing bike setup. Off the showroom floor, a modern sport bike works exceedingly well, but if you jab at the front brake, every set of fork springs will feel too soft. Get your bike in the ballpark, and then work on your riding. Ignore the desire to blame the hardware, and look to the software—yourself—for answers.

11. Riding another student's pace or racing in practice. Testosterone is probably the leading cause of crashes, and I can't fix it with a few words. But I can remind you to focus on riding well—riding within your limits—and the speed/racing thing will take care of itself. Don't get caught up in someone else's bad lines, late entrances and competitive nature.

CHAPTER 9

URBAN SURVIVAL

RIDING TO WORK AGAIN AND AGAIN

I have lived in the Los Angeles area since 1984, and my daily commute from the San Fernando Valley into Hollywood has forced me to study the art of surviving city traffic on a motorcycle. City riders must contend with drivers' moods, slippery intersections, poorly maintained cars and a multitude of unexpected situations. Still, it's too bad only a minority of the thousands of motorcycles registered in America are being used to commute to work or school, because when properly piloted, motorcycles are a great way to get through the city.

Being able to control your motorcycle is an excellent start to surviving in the city, so basic riding skills such as stopping and steering should be sharp. But there are some critical survival points that a rider must always keep in mind: Constantly scan traffic, learn to predict traffic flow, make sure you can be seen, never ride in motorists' blind spots and always have an escape route—a plan in case a car around you does something unexpected.

This chapter is prompted by more than a personal desire to see bikes replace cars for the daily commute. On a wider scale, increased usage of motorcycles to commute would help curb America's energy consumption, reduce pollution, increase the availability of parking spaces and even save wear and tear on the country's highways. Certainly motorcycles are easier to park and they get better mileage than most cars, and the pollution-reduction argument comes from the assumption that traffic flow would improve with more motorcyclists, reducing the amount of air pollution

created by cars idling in traffic jams. In my own case, a typical motorcycle commute lasted between one-half and two-thirds as long as the same commute in a car, meaning the engine getting me to work was polluting for less time, twice a day. And as catalytic converters become more common on two-wheelers, the case for motorcycle commuting gains strength.

FEW ARGUMENTS

There are few arguments against riding a motorcycle in city traffic, but those few carry quite a bit of weight. Chief among them is the danger to life and limb, whether from inattentive car drivers or the "might makes right" mentality that prevails when there is a thoughtless driver behind the wheel. Bike riders must be concerned with weather, parking lot crime and dressing for the conflicting needs of the job and the ride, but their main concern is simply surviving the commute, the trip to the store or the ride to the concert. However, my many years commuting through the heaviest traffic in Los Angeles taught me that urban riding can be predictable, manageable

Left: OK, you're riding "in the mirrors" of the car next to you. Good, but don't make the mistake of assuming that this driver will actually check the mirror before snapping a lane change. Assumptions can be painful. (Brian Blades)

Above right: Greys and browns make up the urban landscape, so you must do everything to be seen. Yellow jacket, multicolored helmet and headlight on make this rider conspicuous. From a visibility standpoint, the ubiquitous black leather jacket is the worst commuting choice, second only to camouflage military fatigues. (Brian Blades)

and survivable. This chapter will examine the risks and arm you with the necessary riding skills and mental ingenuity to survive this highly difficult arena.

You can practice your motorcycle survival techniques as you drive your car. Pretend you're on two wheels with only your skill, wits and riding gear to defend you. Pay attention to your physical relationship with other cars, and how other drivers see you, if they even do. Start thinking like a motorcycle rider before you get on that bike.

START WITH SKILL

To begin, study your bike-control skills, especially your ability to brake. There will be a time when your ability to stop your bike in the shortest possible distance will save your life as surely as your ability to spot a drunk driver. Studies have shown that motorcyclists sometimes make the wrong decision when confronted with a surprise in traffic, for example, they lock the brakes or simply fail to steer around an object they could have easily avoided. Throw a novice into an AMA national race and the results will almost surely be cata-

strophic, and I feel entering heavy traffic without strong basic riding skills is equally dangerous.

Get in the habit of practicing your panic braking often. Do it every ride. The editors I worked with at motorcycle magazines were never on the same bike more than a few days in a row, so we had to explore and learn each motorcycle's braking ability. We would check for traffic behind us and then make a good, hard stop at the next stop sign or red light. We learned to cover the brake lever with our right middle and index fingers at all times, reducing the reaction time when confronted with a surprise. Our minds would constantly appraise the traction situation, and we learned to avoid the slippery middle of the lane when possible. Fluid dripping out of cars usually finds its way to the middle of every traffic lane, while car tires keep the edges of every lane quite clean. Learn to ride on the outside one-third of the lane for maximum traction.

DRESS WELL AND WATCH YOUR SPEED

If you see a motorcycle magazine guy riding to work, he will be dressed well for the riding environment. He knows his protective gear can't be too hot or he'll quit wearing it, yet it has to handle a variety of weather conditions during the weekly commute. Most of the editors wore full-coverage, padded nylon riding suits zipped over their street clothes, like the Aerostich. So if you want to emulate the editors, wear your gear.

And we magazine guys did one other thing: We respected the in-town speed limits. Speed doesn't kill, but it sure adds distance to reactions. Anytime you find yourself freaked out by city traffic, I bet you're well over 45 mph. That's like running down the supermarket aisle looking for Campbell's Tomato Bisque—your speed doesn't give you enough time to read the labels. Speeding in town doesn't give you enough time to read and respond to traffic, and reading traffic is the key to survival. One thing's clear: Slow down in town.

THE SCANNING SKILL

Learning to use your eyes effectively is essential to riding safely in traffic. The moment the eyes stop moving and fixate on a particular car, sign or pedestrian, you've lost your ability to see the big picture, and a painful surprise can follow.

Above left: Riding in the freeway's right lane places you directly in the way of drivers lunging across two lanes to make a last-second exit. Just as bad, you will have to deal with all the traffic merging onto the freeway. Use the right lane for your entrance and exit only, not as a travel lane. (Nick Ienatsch)

Left: The cleanest line through a gravel-strewn corner will be in the tire tracks of a car, and so will the cleanest pavement in town. Here's a typical city lane with gravel, car parts, grease and coolant collected in the middle. Avoid the center of the lane, particularly at traffic lights and tollbooths, where fluids collect from the stopped cars. (Dennis Morrison)

When you're riding in town, the eyes must keep scanning, checking, moving, darting—feeding the brain information about lurking dangers, paths of escape and upcoming problems. Sure, you'll also be listening for horns, sirens and traffic sounds and using your nose to smell diesel spills, but in most instances, your eyes will serve as your primary warning system.

If you listen to enough crash stories, you'll often hear the words, "I was tired, and…" Tired eyes gaze at one object too long. They remain locked on a single possible danger while the motorcycle continues forward toward untold others, and this narrow focus fails to pick up a problem early enough to react to it. Since we'll all occasionally ride when we're tired, it's important to realize the laziness of tired eyes and to make the concerted effort to move those eyes. If you practice scanning when you're fresh, the habit will become a permanent part of your riding, even when commuting home at midnight.

SHOULD EVERYONE RIDE A BIKE? NO!

Frankly, some car drivers should never ride a motorcycle in traffic. I'm frequently asked by concerned parents/spouses if their loved one would be safe riding a bike in traffic, and judging a driver's habits in a car helps to gauge his or her risk on a bike. Apply this test to any driver who wants to become a rider:

1. Are you always being encroached upon by other drivers? If so, you're driving in too many blind spots and are unaware of how to "drive in someone's mirrors."

2. Do you honk your horn daily just to survive? Your horn should be your last line of defense. If you constantly rely on it to get through traffic safely, you aren't reading traffic patterns well, and you're in the wrong place—probably in someone else's blind spot.

3. Is every other driver on the road out to get you? It's okay to think they're out to get you, but drivers who really believe it drive in a timid manner. They don't maintain their place in the flow of traffic, and are constantly taken advantage of by more aggressive drivers.

4. Does stopped traffic frequently surprise you, forcing you to brake hard every time you drive? If so, your eyes are too low and you aren't looking far enough ahead of your car.

5. Do you have trouble accelerating onto a freeway to merge smoothly with traffic? You won't survive on a motorcycle without a good deal of aggression and an ability to fit into traffic smoothly.

6. Are you honked at often? Drivers who get honked at usually aren't paying attention, are daydreaming at traffic lights

or are changing lanes without looking or signaling. If you can't stay totally focused on your driving, don't try riding.

7. Are you constantly the recipient of road rage? Drivers get angry when their safety is threatened, and recipients of road rage are often doing something that distorts the normal flow of traffic badly enough to endanger lives.

8. Do you drive below the posted speed limit for safety? Those who do have no idea of how traffic really flows and are confusing speed with safety, a mistake that will have tough consequences on a motorcycle.

9. Do you neglect your turn signal switch? Communicating with other drivers reduces surprises, and your turn signal is a primary source of communication. If you don't use it in your car, you aren't truly working with traffic around you.

10. Do you believe everyone on the road is crazy and that it's only a matter of time before one of these crazy drivers hits you? If you feel accidents are inevitable and your turn is coming, stay in that Volvo station wagon.

If you answered yes to one or two questions, you might be trainable. If you answered yes to more than a few, you may not enjoy or survive a motorcycle in traffic. It's okay to be paranoid and believe that everyone on the road is poorly trained, but if that outlook distracts you from what you're doing at the handlebar, then you must realign your priorities to quit worrying about aspects you can't control and totally master those you can.

BE A TRUCK, BE A BICYCLE

Drivers of Mack trucks have a significantly different view of city traffic than do bicycle riders. The truck driver bulls through traffic, while the bicycle rider sneaks. The trucker demands the right of way, but the bicycle rider concedes it quickly. The truck driver automatically assumes that everyone sees him, and the bicycle rider assumes she's invisible. To be a safe and successful inner-city motorcyclist, you need to combine elements of both of these contrasting approaches to driving.

We've all been told to "ride defensively," but in the real world a purely defensive rider simply gets taken advantage of, pushed around, ignored and possibly run over. The aggressive rider is in equal danger but for different reasons. The aggressive rider doesn't realize that car drivers constantly make mistakes, and his aggressiveness puts him in harm's way too often. You must find the balance between aggressive and defensive riding, and it's that balance that the truck driver/bicycle rider analogy speaks to. As you read farther, keep this relationship in mind. Occupy your space like the truck driver, but concede like the bicyclist.

MOVING THROUGH TRAFFIC

Part of your aggressiveness must be a conscious effort to move through traffic, not just to flow with it. The California Highway Patrol teaches its motorcycle officers to ride slightly faster than traffic because it places them in better control of the situation and less open to others' mistakes. It also reduces the risk of errant car drivers approaching you from the rear and allows you to concentrate a bit more on the right, left and forward situations. Now, this means riding only slightly faster than surrounding traffic and picking your way through the mess, not blasting past with 15 mph in hand. You simply want to be slightly aggressive, not overtly illegal.

Many riders are concerned with speed and following distances, when their first priority should be conspicuousness. In fact, I would speed or tailgate in order to clear a car's blind spot and reach a place where the surrounding cars can actually see me. Many novice motorcyclists assume they can be seen, and their assumption is often mistaken and can carry a high cost.

Blind spot awareness is paramount. The same alarm that warns you of cold tires on the racetrack should also be sounding when you get into another vehicle's blind spot. You can tell when you're in a blind spot because you can't see the driver's head in his rear-view mirrors. And if you can't see him, guess what—that's right, he can't see you. Move quickly to a point where you can see the driver's head in the mirror so that he has a fighting chance of seeing you before changing lanes. Never assume that a driver will actually use his mirrors, but be in them at all times.

LEARNING CARS

No two vehicles have similar blind spots due to differences in vehicle design, driver height, mirror adjustment and other factors. Every vehicle is a new exercise in the art of riding in the mirrors. One glance at a car carrying four people should set off an alarm, because the driver's inside mirror may be blocked by the extra heads in the back seat. One glance at a gardening truck with a missing right outside mirror should scare you away. A car full of balloons is basically mirrorless. A custom Chevy truck with cute little mirrors and a boat behind it should get your attention. As you scan traffic, you should also notice any badly adjusted mirrors. Use the throttle to get clear of these rolling blind spots, and if you can't

THE TRUCK

Making yourself as visible as a truck is a fascinating objective, involving mirrors, lane position, vehicle type, driver type, blind spots, road conditions, following distances, mental outlook and even time of day. The basic objective is to be conspicuous, while believing that nobody sees you—ever. Everything from your riding gear to your headlight to your lane position to your thumb on the horn button is aimed at getting you seen, noticed, observed. You can learn to position your motorcycle in such a way that it is as obvious as a truck. You must learn to make yourself seen.

THE BICYCLE

You can pretend you're a truck, but in reality you must realize you are only a bicyclist. Act like a truck by putting your bike where it should be and working within the confines of traffic flow. Remember, though, that the right of way may be yours but you can't insist on it. You must learn to give way when seriously challenged, avoid confrontation and be constantly aware. You must always expect the worst so you'll be prepared when it happens.

get ahead of them, make sure that your lane position keeps you clear of their next mistake. These skills will become second nature if you work at them every time you ride or drive.

THE BLIND SPOT AND THE DEATH SPOT

Within every blind spot is a death spot, a place where you will be in harm's way if that vehicle changes lanes or encroaches on your space. Learn to avoid the death spot no matter what. As you move through traffic, remember that as soon as your front wheel draws parallel with a vehicle's rear bumper you are in the death spot, and you will remain in the death spot until you are fully past the vehicle. Like the blind spot, the location and size of the death spot varies, and it can even depend upon the performance of the vehicle. After all, a 1974 GMC van probably can't whip a lane change as quickly as a Lotus Esprit, yet the van's death spot is considerably longer than the Esprit's.

A rider is often forced into blind spots by other cars, especially in heavy, multilane traffic where the pace of your lane can stall you in the blind spot of a car in the next lane.

Left: The trucker occupies space confidently, taking for granted that other drivers see him. The bicyclist slips along the edges of traffic, relying on his maneuverability and constantly evolving escape plan. A motorcyclist must ride with the trucker's confidence and sense of purpose, yet have the bicyclist's agility to slip past problems. (Dennis Morrison)

Below: This Oversize Load has no idea you're behind it because your lane placement puts you out of his mirrors. Use the width of your lane to keep yourself in the mirrors of the cars surrounding you. Don't be a passenger/victim. Ride your bike and place it conspicuously and defensively in traffic. (Dennis Morrison)

Do anything to get visible, whether that means slowing slightly to fall into the car's mirrors, or accelerating closer to the vehicle in front of you to pull next to the driver in the adjacent lane. It might mean adjusting your lane position a bit, pulling closer to the car in the next lane to gain a spot in his mirrors, or moving farther away as you enter the death spot to gain time and distance should the car lurch into your lane. Learn to spend as little time as possible in the death spot. An alarm should be going off in your head every time you enter the death spot, and this alarm should not be quelled until you clear the death spot. Riding well in traffic is a constant adjustment of speed and lane position, requiring the same total concentration needed while lapping a racetrack.

THE RIGHT LANE POSITION ISN'T ALWAYS LEFT

Many experts will tell you to ride in the left third of the lane, and in most instances this is good advice. When you place yourself in the left side of the lane, the driver in front of you has a chance of seeing you in her left and inside mirror, should she bother to look. However, if you lock yourself into one lane position, you could be cheating yourself out of being more conspicuous, especially to a car ahead of you on the right. So get in the habit of using the whole lane to your advantage, moving into mirrors when possible and away from cars when necessary. On a multilane freeway, it makes sense to ride wherever a leading car can see you for as long as it's safe, then move across the lane as you enter that car's

blind spot to give you a buffer zone in case it makes a quick lane change. That extra eight feet can make a huge difference. My final thought on lane position is do whatever puts you in the mirrors of the cars around you, and as far away as possible when those cars make mistakes.

EVERY FIVE SECONDS

Inner-city riders learn to check their mirrors often—like every five seconds. That's a good habit, and learning to check your turn-signal switch at the same time is a great habit. I believe that uncanceled turn signals are responsible for more accidents than you can imagine. Most bikes have push-to-cancel switches, so get in the habit of canceling your turn signal every time you check your mirrors. That's every five seconds. Look and push.

Some riders, afraid of leaving their turn signals flashing inadvertently, decide to quit using them entirely. Bad decision. Use those signals to communicate your intentions to everyone around you, whether it's a lane change or a left turn. Turn signals help draw attention to your bike, adding conspicuousness as well as helping traffic flow. There have been many times my flashing turn signal caught the attention of the driver ahead, holding

him in place while I moved left or right. Without the signal, that driver would have assumed that I was staying put behind him, and we could have ended up fighting for the same piece of open pavement to our left or right. Guess who wins?

And while we're talking about control switches, use the high beam of your headlight to raise your profile in town during daylight hours, but flip to low beam when you're going to be behind a certain vehicle for any length of time. Some drivers get quite irritated when a bike's high beam is burning a hole in their retinas, so go to low beam to keep the irritation level down. Yes, this means thumbing your switch many times during a morning commute, but remember, this is an action sport.

YOUR BLIND SPOT AND MIRROR MEMORIZATION

Although most threats will come from the front or sides, you

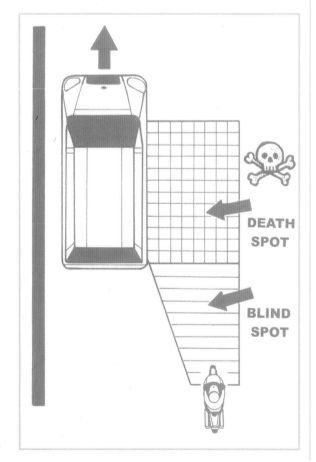

Left: Blind spots change depending upon the vehicle, but be especially aware (read *paranoid*) when you enter the death spot, the area parallel to the car, truck or van. An alarm should sound in your helmet anytime you find yourself in this position on an urban ride. Use your throttle, lane position and total alertness to stay clear of the death spot. (Hector Cademartori)

Above: This rider is well placed in the right side of the lane, in position to see changes in the flow of traffic because trouble to his right will have an immediate effect on the High Occupancy Vehicle lane. Anticipating problems early and having a plan to avoid these types of situations is just as important as finely honed physical riding skills. (Nick Ienatsch)

Above right: Turn signals are great communicators. This rider plans a pass to the left of the car in the middle lane. The early use of the turn signal helps freeze that driver in the center lane, assuming the driver checks his mirrors. Use your turn signals religiously and cancel them as frequently as you check your mirrors—every five seconds. (Hector Cademartori)

Below right: Danger! This guy's left hand is busy holding his cell phone, so don't expect him to use a turn signal. His mind is elsewhere, so don't expect his actions to be remotely predictable. A secret to urban riding is spotting cell-phone users early and staying clear. This is especially important when splitting lanes, because cell-phone users tend to drift in their lane and not watch their mirrors. (Gary Lehman)

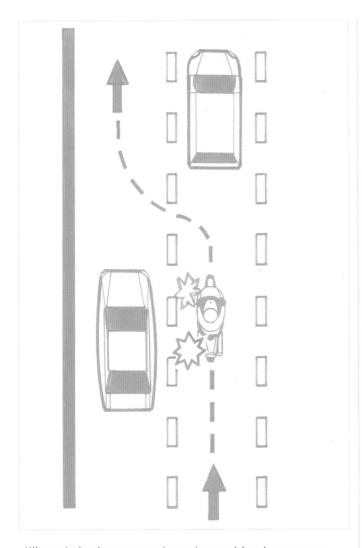

a bit of acceleration to burst ahead of any car lurking next to you might save you a peek in the mirror at a critical time. This technique isn't as safe as a glance over your shoulder, but there are times when taking your eyes off what's ahead simply isn't possible.

To be sure you have instant acceleration, you should learn to ride your bike in its powerband in heavy traffic. (A motorcycle's powerband is the engine rpm range where the bike makes good, strong power.) Loafing along at 2500 rpm might be okay in your V8 pickup, but your bike must be in a position to respond to throttle input immediately. When you hear magazine writers talk about dangerously slow, under-performing motorcycles, they mean bikes that don't have the power to clear a blind spot or fill a hole in traffic. If you're in the market for a commuting bike, opt for a machine with strong mid-range torque to keep you clear of trouble with just a twist of throttle at any rpm.

Riding your bike in its powerband will require you to add another skill to your repertoire: flashing your brake light during deceleration. Because of the high rpm and compression of a motorcycle engine, off-throttle can result in considerable slowing, especially compared to a heavy car with an automatic transmission. Any time you roll off the throttle with a car behind you, flash your brake light with your fingers or your foot, even though you're not braking. The flashing light might get the driver's attention and let him know you are slowing quickly. Then again, it might not, so keep checking those mirrors and be ready to take evasive action, like pulling up next to the car in front of you.

BEYOND BLIND SPOTS

Mastering blind spots and avoiding death spots requires constant and precise speed adjustments. To be fully prepared to make these adjustments, one of your city survival skills must be driver identification. This means understanding not only

still must check your rearview mirrors at least once every five seconds. Prior to a lane change, a look over your shoulder is the safest and best method to ensure a clear lane, but there are times in heavy traffic when a long gaze in the mirror or a look over your shoulder isn't possible. Learn to glance quickly in your mirror and then return your attention up front, while mentally recalling what your mirror revealed. This is called *mirror memorization,* and you can learn to do it with just a quick movement of your eyes, taking a snapshot of your mirror and keeping your attention forward as much as possible as your mind recalls the snapshot. As you master this technique, these frequent snapshots will blend into a movie that tells the story behind you without requiring a large time commitment. Spend some time practicing the Vision Revision eye drills in chapter 3. They will help you develop the vision and memorization skills you need, and you can practice them anywhere, not just when you're on your bike and your life is at stake.

A motorcycle's blind spot can be quite large, depending upon the mirrors and their adjustment. If you find yourself in a situation where a look over your shoulder isn't possible, think of your throttle as a blind-spot clearance tool, because

who is behind the wheel of a given car, but also what sort of vehicle it is and how it is being driven. Identify the types that bully you, the types that ignore you, the types that really don't see you, the types that want to work with you and the types that won't ever give you space. Whom can you trust? Whom can you tailgate? Whom can't you intimidate? Who is clueless? You must begin to form general rules to help you determine your actions when presented with a variety of drivers and cars.

Over the years, I've learned to respect young men in four-wheel drive trucks. They rise immediately to a challenge, they don't want to be tailgated and you can't intimidate them on a motorcycle. Fine, I offer them respectful following distances and keep them mollified with unchallenging riding.

I've learned that a junk car usually means a junk driver. If a person doesn't have enough automotive enthusiasm to keep their car clean, they haven't spent the time to perfect their driving either. Get past them and don't get close, because junk cars usually have no insurance.

Anytime I see a vehicle with a company logo on the side, I see a careless driver. Since there's been no personal money spent on the vehicle, the driver couldn't care less about how they drive it or how many scratches are accumulated.

An out-of-state plate or obvious rental car should set off

Right: The sun refracting in the camera lens illustrates the problems of sunrise and sunset commuting, which are a further challenge to undertrained drivers. Think about the sun's position during these busy times, especially when approaching intersections, and remember that drivers are distracted by the glare and will have an even harder time spotting you. (Dennis Morrison)

Below: This is what trouble looks like, in addition to a million other problems that prevent us from being clearly seen. Learn to spot and avoid homemade campers and other vehicles with mile-long blind spots. (Nick Ienatsch)

alarms, because the direction of travel may radically change at a moment's notice. If the person driving has no idea where they're going, how can you?

Pay attention to the backseat driver or the passenger issuing directions. You'll see a hand gesture from the passenger just before the car lunges for a right turn from the left lane. In fact, any time you see lots of talking and gesturing in a car around you, know that little attention is being paid to the motorcycles in the area.

Pay attention to anyone driving a large car with too much caution and defensiveness. They are scared. They have been in accidents before, they are certain that accidents are unavoidable, so they buy the biggest or safest car on the market and drive it well below the killing speed limit. Their first reaction to any situation will be braking, so don't get caught behind them. They will never use their mirrors, so don't get beside them. It's better to be well in front of them.

Give older drivers room. In general, they don't see too well, their reactions are slower and they need some understanding. Most older drivers have realized that speed is no longer a priority, and they probably don't care about the things they can't see. That means you on your motorcycle.

Cell-phone users will get you simply because they will never see you. Be prepared for cell-phone users to be late on the brakes, late on the gas, slow to recognize everything around them and completely oblivious to anything beyond the handset. Don't expect turn signals either…their hands are too busy!

Whom can you trust? Nobody. The moment you place your life in another's hands, you're done. Even though there might be a few driver types I trust a little bit, we motorcyclists must learn to trust only ourselves. Trust sometimes brings complacency, and there's no room for that when you're moving down the road.

The ability to see and identify driver types is part of the aggressiveness you need to survive. You must instantly react to the general stereotypes you see, but be ready to modify your stereotype at a moment's notice, especially if you encounter the little old lady from Pasadena of Beach Boys fame, the grandma who "drives real fast and drives real hard" (God bless her!). In other parts of life, relying on stereotypes is often foolhardy, but motorcyclists can generally assume the worst about other drivers and then work from there.

THE GAME OF READING TRAFFIC

Holding your own on the highway means reading traffic flow and knowing where each car fits and plans to be in the immediate future. Try to learn the area in which you are riding and identify the usual problem spots that will create congestion or confusion. For instance, if it's 7:45

a.m. and you're leaving your neighborhood, it's safe to assume most drivers are commuting to work and will be headed to the freeway. Time of day becomes a huge issue when you consider the sun's position early in the morning and late in the afternoon. If you're eastbound at sunset, assume you are invisible to anyone waiting to pull out in front of you. Scan and identify anything that ultimately affects you, whether it's traffic entering a crowded freeway three lanes away or a line of cars waiting to turn left against the traffic in your lane.

Reading traffic becomes a game you can play any time you're on the road, whether piloting two wheels or four. The trick is to guess what cars are going to do before they do it. You will learn that a car that tailgates is about to pop a lane change. Out-of-state plates will make mistakes at every freeway diversion. Certain drivers in certain cars will always put on their brakes, not accelerate, to change lanes. An impatient driver waiting to pull out in traffic will soon get desperate.

Figure out how traffic will mesh together as the right lane ends. When you see a left hand move toward the turn signal switch, a lane change is coming. A hurried glance over the shoulder signals a hurried lane change, and if you study these moves carefully you'll soon spot lane changes well before the turn signal flashes, if it's used at all. Older driv-ers may have trouble looking over their shoulder, so expect a blind lane change, and don't be there when it happens.

GETTING OUT

The traffic-reading game will teach you an important aspect of urban survival: Always have an out. While you're scanning and observing, part of your brain must be busy planning escape routes, places you can fit your motorcycle if the worst comes. Many times your way out will be an aggressive braking maneuver, but it can also be hard acceleration or fit-ting yourself between two lanes of cars. Use your imagination to create possible problems, like those logs slip-ping off the back of that flatbed, and then imagine where you would go to miss the carnage. You will soon learn to place yourself in a position that will allow you to miss the problems you're imagining.

The game of reading traffic must become second nature. Like all games, you'll learn to keep score, and as you can guess, the mistakes can have significant consequences. Get in the habit of scoring your game harshly. If you are sur-prised by something, examine where your attention was just prior to the surprise. What type of vehicle and driver was it? Were there any clues that could have tipped you off, clues that you missed? If the surprise was so unexpected that you were in danger or had to make emergency avoidance

horn button and your fingers and foot covering the brakes. Slow down and enjoy the fact that you're even moving!

LESSONS FROM THE RACETRACK

TOTAL FOCUS The best roadracers exhibit an intense concentration and focus on their riding. Take that principle and apply it to your in-town riding. Don't be distracted by anything that pulls your mind from the task of traffic survival.

PASS TECH Roadracers are known for their exceptional bike preparation, and we street riders need to be aware of this as well. Pretend your bike must pass technical inspection before it's ridden to work, and if it's not up to snuff, leave it home until the problem is corrected.

GET GOOD Racers practice a lot. So should you. When that minivan dodges into your path, your riding skills must be ultra-sharp because the consequences are actually harsher on the street than they are on the racetrack.

RIDE SOBER It's a shame to have to mention it, but don't drink and ride. If you have a wild office party planned, make arrangements to leave your bike at the office and get a ride home. Roadracers train hard, eat right and do nothing to add to the difficulty of our sport. Do the same for your commute.

NO BRAKE LIGHTS Roadracing bikes don't have brake lights...and plenty of cars out there don't either! Learn to judge speed and deceleration without relying on brake lights.

Above: Like a roadracer, this commuter must live in the future by getting the eyes up to scan, predict traffic movements and constantly reassess the environment. Downtown rush-hour commuting makes roadracing seem easy. (Brian Blades)

Right: Racetrack tech inspections are serious and are to ensure safety as much as they are to enforce compliance with the rules. Your inspections should be serious too, and cleaning your bike is an important part of that. A tech inspector won't even look at a dirty bike because grime hides problems liked cracked brake rotors or leaking seals. (Brian J. Nelson)

maneuvers, you must come away with a lesson that will help you notice the next similar instance. Playing this game keeps you in tune with everything around you and, more importantly, keeps you prepared for whatever your immediate future holds.

CALIFORNIA LANE SHARING

Many of you either live in California or will ride in California sometime, so it's important to discuss lane sharing, or lane splitting, as it's commonly known. The rules behind this practice are a bit tough to pin down, but understand that the California Highway Patrol (CHP) regards lane sharing as a "good thing" because it reduces congestion. Every rider I know is thankful for lane sharing, so it's important that we don't abuse it to the point we can no longer enjoy it legally.

The CHP wants lane sharing to take place between the number one and number two freeway lanes (the lane farthest to the left is the number one lane), and at speeds no faster than 10 mph above the speed of traffic, and never over the posted speed limit. California car drivers have learned to expect and respect motorcyclists riding between the one and two lanes, and you will be surprised at the amount of room almost everyone gives you. An occasional uptight driver will fail to move over, but it's hardly an issue anymore. The true danger is that many motorcyclists ride far too fast between traffic, and when the unexpected happens, there's no room or time to react.

The trouble comes when a car lunges toward an open spot in the adjoining lane, so learn to be on double-alert any time you're approaching an opening in traffic on either side of you. Ride with your high beam on, your thumb covering the

Solving the Problem

Next time you're in a conversation with someone who thinks lane sharing should be legislated out of existence, make sure they understand that without lane sharing, things would be even worse. All the motorcycles currently used for commuting would join the ranks of cars parked on the freeway. Motorcycle commuters are the solution, not the problem.

CHAPTER 10

GROUP RIDING AND THE PACE
SOME COMMON SENSE THAT ISN'T COMMON ENOUGH

Your phone rings and a guy you faintly remember from school invites you on a group sport ride to the café in a neighboring town. Do you go?

Many of you wouldn't. You've ridden with relative strangers before, and it's always been a crapshoot of stupid passes, blind-spot following distances, ill-timed wheelies and the constant sense that disaster is waiting around the next corner. Perhaps one of your group rides has ended by the side of the road as you haul one of the gang up the embankment and then head home to get your truck. You thank your school friend, decline his invitation and end up riding alone the next day.

Don't get me wrong, riding alone can be hugely rewarding, but many agree that the camaraderie of riding with the right group beats riding alone any day.

So how do you find the right group? You make it.

COMMUNICATION IS THE KEY
Think about two of the most common types of groups in our lives: families and co-workers. In both situations, communication is the key to success. The same ability to talk about

problems and solutions is exactly what is needed in a riding group. Communication within a riding group takes two forms: verbal and physical.

VERBAL COMMUNICATION: SOME SUGGESTIONS
The verbal communication comes first, before the ride even starts. "Where are we going? Do you want to take the 120 cut-off or just run on the freeway to Hudson Street? Pat, why don't you lead because most of us have never been there before. Hey, be aware of the fact that my brake light bulb just burned out." That's communication in a very simple form, and it serves to get everyone going in the same direction and talking about the ride. But it's not nearly enough.

Keep talking. "Who wants to lead going out of Marysville? Okay, John, after you lead awhile, wave someone else by so you don't hog the lead. Whoever is leading when we get on that long downhill before the bridge, look out for radar. Let's swap the lead every five miles or so. Keep an eye on Todd because he's brand new. And Todd, be mellow and ride your own pace."

Then start talking about the important things.

Left: Welcome to an enjoyable, sustainable street ride. We know it's the street because of the centerline, oncoming traffic, trees and guardrails at road's edge and—just as significant—by the distinct lack of competition between three friends. The pace is quick and fun, but at least 30 percent off a race pace. (Jeff Allen)

Right: Riding in foreign countries puts an emphasis on careful map reading, but life gets easier when the group follows one simple rule: No matter what, follow the current leader until you can safely stop and discuss the situation. The day gets awfully long when riders try to lead from the back! (Brian Blades)

The original *Sport Rider* magazine editorial staff talked about group riding all the time, because we rode together all the time. When you're riding with your friends, don't be afraid to discuss mistakes, speed, routes, environment and the beautiful view. (Wes Allison, courtesy of *Sport Rider*)

Offer suggestions and opinions. "I think the best way to do this is to ride in a staggered formation with the leader on the left side of the lane. In the twisties, everyone uses the whole lane, but give the rider ahead of you some room, okay? When we get into town, close up the formation so we can all make the lights. When we get out on Highway 12 we might come up on slower traffic, so make sure each of us has a clear pass. Look for an opening. Don't pass just because the rider ahead of you passes. Remember what happened to Chuck."

Get that dialogue started. If you ride with a group or want to ride with a group, this chapter will provide you with an excellent blueprint. But it all depends on communication.

PHYSICAL COMMUNICATION: SOME SUGGESTIONS

I grew up riding with my dad in the Salt Lake City Motorcycle Club, and our president, Larry Chidester, taught the whole club some great hand signals that I've incorporated with the Motorcycle Safety Foundation hand signals. The leader initiates most of the communication and it's passed up or down the line to all riders.

Left arm out, forearm straight down, palm backward: Stop.

Left hand pointing or right foot off peg: Hazard in road, caution.

One finger held up: Single file.

Two fingers held up: Double file, staggered.

Left arm out, palm up, moving up and down: Speed up.

Left arm out, palm down, moving up and down: Slow down.

Left arm up, palm forward: I'm leading, follow me.

Left arm swinging horizontally with index finger out: Pass me.

Tapping top of helmet: Your high beam is on.

Left arm out, hand opening and closing: Your turn signal is on.

Left hand up, pointing overhead back and forth: We're pulling off.

Left elbow out, index finger pointing to tank: I need fuel.

Left elbow out, thumb pointing toward mouth: I need refreshment.

Left fist out: I need a bathroom break.

SET SOME RULES

When everyone is on the same song sheet, the music is prettier. The song sheet for a group ride depends upon who is singing. Rules can add safety to the ride, and at the very least, they help you avoid future hassles.

As the years add up, certain rules have proven to save lives and hassle. Like staying to the right of the centerline except to pass. Like passing only when you see that it's clear. Like limiting straight-line speed to a preset limit. Like following the leader. Like never passing a fellow group rider until you are signaled past on the left. Like waving to everyone who moves over for you on a mountain road. Like waiting for everyone on the straights, where speed is too easy and cops too plentiful.

Which brings us to The Pace.

THE PACE

The Pace was invented one day when *Motorcyclist* editor Mitch Boehm and I were lost in the Santa Monica Mountains and hit upon a fun style of riding. We were both on the latest, greatest sport bikes that were equally at home on the racetrack, but we both knew well that racetrack speeds were deadly on the street. The most common solo street-bike crash comes from too much speed entering a corner, and a ton of straightaway speed is usually the reason the entrance gets blown. Many riders learn how to accelerate aggressively, but their braking and trail-braking techniques aren't up to par, resulting in a ruined and disastrous corner entrance.

The rhythm that Mitch and I had fallen into was this: cool on the straights and fun in the corners. When we analyzed our new technique, which I coined "The Pace," we saw that our straightaway speeds were relatively low compared to what the bikes were capable of doing. Another reason for these slower speeds was our ticket situation, which wasn't particularly admirable at the time. Think about it: Big speed usually happens in a straight line, and the police have that figured out. Our new pace took away that straight-line throttle-happiness and saved the fun for the corners, with occasional full-throttle blasts up freeway on-ramps. After all, straight-line speed is easy and boring compared to a perfectly clipped apex.

THE PACE AND THE GROUP

As The Pace permeated our riding, it rubbed off on the group we rode with. The straight sections became a chance to relax and actually look at the scenery a bit, but more importantly, to reset the ranks of the group. We'd often use the straights to trade the lead or simply giggle about the last set of corners or the ones coming up. This is the exact opposite of racing, a venue where nobody waits for you.

Because the lead changes frequently, the pace of the group does too. Remember, if you can't follow the leader, no one will follow your lead. A slower leader just means you can relax and work on all the things addressed in the previous chapters, while a quick leader means the straights will work perfectly to reform the group.

As you've learned all through this book, rushing the entrance of corners just doesn't work. It doesn't work on the track and it doesn't work on the street. If you stick to real-world speed on the straight parts, the next corner will come at you at speeds right at your ability. In fact, you will enjoy street riding so much more when you eliminate the race-track speeds. Trust me. I've been at the top of the AMA SuperTeams and 250GP ranks, and racetrack speed is simply not manageable on the street.

The Pace allows you to focus on the corners, and that means line selection, trail-braking, early throttle application—all the things discussed in previous chapters. The Pace allows you to enjoy the best part of your modern motorcycle without putting yourself in constant danger at every corner entrance and at every radar trap.

A good way to regulate the speed of your group is to discuss speed limits and then set a maximum speed. You might be on a road with some long, fast sections that can be ridden quickly, but because a few of the turns are blind, it's dangerous to traverse that section at 120 mph. (At 120 mph, you're covering 176 feet every second. Yikes!) You might want to agree to running no more than 75 mph on the straight, boring stuff. Setting an agreed-to speed limit helps keep the group intact and the pace sane. If you happen to tag onto the back of the group I ride with, you'll rarely, if ever, ride over 75 mph on the straight sections. My survival and love of street riding comes from an adherence to this concept of controlled speed.

Left: Magazine photo shoots aren't immune from crashes, so the *Sportbike* staff puts the bikes close together in a staggered formation, allowing each rider total use of the lane if necessary. This is also a safe way to ride through the city. When you ride in a staggered formation, you see more and you have an "out" if the rider ahead of you stops quickly or unexpectedly, for example, at a light that turns from green to yellow. You don't need to work at a magazine to develop a cohesive riding group. (Brian Blades)

Below: This shot illustrates the use of the straight to regroup the riders. Rather than haul ass down the boring straight part, the leaders slow to tighten the gang before tipping into the next right-hander. The group naturally strings out due to riding speeds, but a race doesn't start because everyone recognizes the straights are for regrouping. (Jeff Allen)

THIS AIN'T A RACE

Riding with friends means keeping an eye on your friends. If you haven't seen your buddy in the mirror for two miles or two minutes, slow until you do. If everyone does this, the group will naturally stay together. Not only does this keep the group together, but it will save valuable time in case one rider does have a problem and needs help.

If you're riding with a group that makes every ride a race, get away from them right now. Have them read chapter 8 on getting on the racetrack, and don't listen to all the excuses they will have for not racing. The smallest street accident is usually significantly more devastating than any racetrack crash, and riders running a race-pace on the street will crash. You don't want to be there when it happens.

I can guarantee you that I've heard every excuse for not racing. If a guy is riding smart on the street and doesn't want to go racing, that's perfectly fine. But when a street rider is pushing all the time—using a lot of motor and brakes, and riding with a deliberately intense attitude—and then gives reasons for not racing, it's pure BS.

I really valued the group I rode with as we practiced The Pace. There were four of us, sometimes five, and we had a fantastic time. I can remember being the fifth bike in line as we all flicked back and forth through a set of esses, or looking in my mirror to see my friends heeled over in a third-gear sweeper. What a gas. Our pace was truly quick, but not fast. Big difference.

Everyone in my favorite riding group raced or had raced. The skill level was high, but our group dynamic kept the egos in check. The lead changed all the time, and the straights were a chance to cruise one-handed, wave to other riders and cops and save our licenses. We looked forward to corners like dogs wait for dinner, setting our bikes on the exact line and working with inches rather than feet when selecting turn-in points and apexes.

RACERBOY

Our little group was occasionally joined by new riders. Most of them caught on to our approach, especially after a little coaching, but once we had a guy who just didn't get it. We were at the Rock Store and a local Willow racer asked where we were going and could he come along. Sure, we said, and gave him a quick thumbnail of where we were going and how we rode.

In the first canyon, this guy was in the middle of the group and slowly worked his way forward, passed the leader and motored away, hanging off radically and trying pretty hard...in other words, racing us. We all watched and continued to have fun until we got to the top of the canyon and met the guy. None of us were hanging off, tucking in or using much motor.

Well, on the next fun road the same thing happened, and

we simply stopped, turned around and went the other way as Racerboy disappeared in the distance. We wanted to ride together. We wanted to ride with friends. We wanted to go quickly but not fast. And we didn't want to be picking someone out of the grill of a truck on a Southern California back road. I can remember a classic comment from one of our group: "I only race for points and money." None of us needed the hassle on our day off.

The Racerboy story illustrates the need to control the group you ride with. I'll say it again: If you see someone riding over their head, taking unsafe chances, riding unsafe machinery, riding without the right gear, following too closely, etc., mention it and follow up with some solutions or stop riding with them. You'll either improve a friend's

Left: Tucked-in and wheelying...hmmm...what would the sheriff think? Fortunately, there are tracks and track days that welcome this level of intensity more warmly than Officer Petersen does. (Brian Blades)

Above: Here's a fundamental concept: Ride with respect for the other members of your group! That means safe following distances, sane speeds when you're leading and polite passes. Sounds like a recipe for a fun day of riding, and fun is why you bought a bike in the first place. Don't let the wrong group mentality ruin your ride. (Jeff Allen)
Right: Gotta race? Local motocross and desert races are a relatively inexpensive way to flex those competitive muscles. Getting a little crazy here is almost expected, but it's also usually easy to dust yourself off if you crash, and it complements street riding nicely. (Jay McNally)

chance of survival or get rid of the problem altogether.

YOUR SAFETY MARGIN

A big part of The Pace involves leaving yourself a safety margin and a margin for error—whether your own or someone else's. There are too many surprises and unknowns out there, and a rider who has no margin for adjustment of lines or speeds will soon find himself a victim.

Let's listen in on these victims:

"Yeah, I crashed in that right-hander with the gravel in it."
"I fell because that tree branch surprised me."
"That corner tightened up on me and I couldn't make it."
"This piece of junk dragged the centerstand and made me crash."
"I came up on that car so fast, I grabbed the brakes and crashed."

And so on. In every one of these excuses, the rider was too close to the edge of traction, his bike's limits or his own riding abilities. The unexpected happened, and the rider didn't have enough of a margin to deal with it. The result is a crash and a weak excuse.

If you ride at 100 percent on the track, think about knocking at least 30 percent off your aggressiveness when you street ride. If you aren't a track rider, review your riding history and be honest with yourself as you assess the number of times you've exceeded your personal comfort levels. Those are good indications that you have exceeded your safety margin as well. Take the time to find out why you're uncomfortable and then make changes. Discomfort is only a few steps ahead of a crash. It's the closest you'll ever come to someone tapping you on the shoulder and saying, "Hey Bud, you're going to crash if you keep doing that."

YOUR BODY IN THE BREEZE

Think about your riding position on the street. A tucked-in racer's crouch sets off alarm bells in police officers and ordinary citizens, so avoid that track tuck. After all, would you rather cruise past a highway patrolman in a full tuck at 70 mph or just be sitting up in the breeze? I can tell you from experience, the sit-up stance looks a lot more innocent.

And don't hang off radically on the street either. You might want to shift your body slightly to the inside of the corner, but as soon as that butt comes off the seat and your inside knee comes out, I'll bet you're running speeds that are well beyond your 70 percent safety margin. On 49 days out of 50 you might get away with those racing speeds, but that one day when the unexpected happens is a real killer.

And think about what a cop sees. A guy hauling ass toward him with a knee on the ground, or a guy hauling ass toward him in a nice, neat riding position? The knee on the ground on a public road is a ticket to jail and another black mark against everyone involved in our sport.

GROUP RULES TO LIVE BY

Pass one at a time. You make the pass only when you confirm that the way is clear. Trouble happens when one rider blindly follows another. If you establish an "okay to pass" sign, make sure everyone respects how important it is to exercise safe judgment when giving a following rider that sign. You are holding her life in your hands.

When you make a pass, do it smartly. Don't waste time meandering past a car. Pop a downshift or two and move

past the slower vehicle fairly quickly in order to give your fellow riders more time to assess their passing chances. Don't blast past in a full-throttle redline assault; simply move past efficiently and then stretch out a bit ahead of the vehicle to let your friends have room. Nothing is more frustrating than a leader who passes slowly and then rides just ahead of the passed vehicle.

Never touch or cross the centerline, except to pass. Make this a rule right from the beginning to avoid the wildly divergent lines and speeds that can come when riders ignore the centerline. The challenge is riding well on the correct side of the road.

Control your straightaway speeds. Big speed is too easy...for you and the cops. Keep it to a low boil on the straights and live for the turns. The boring straight parts are a great place to regroup your friends. And here's an idea: Look at the scenery!

Talk about it. If you see something you don't like, say something. Communication will either fix the problem or eliminate it.

Don't ride with idiots. In chapter 7 I told a story about a married couple I saw crippled by a notoriously inattentive riding buddy. He always followed too closely, and one day he hit them. He was an idiot, and now they're crippled.

Ride with your friends, not against them. Are you supercompetitive? Me too...so I go to a racetrack when I need to race. Do it, or pay big time.

Practice riding techniques, not racing speeds. I have given you a lifetime of work in this one book, and these skills can be honed at sane street speeds. As I've told students, when the bike is in the right place and you're making the right control inputs, speed comes easily. Trying to go fast with poor technique is a recipe for disaster.

Leave a margin for error. You never know when you'll need it, so have it with you all the time.

Left: Who is that rider right on your rear fender, and how well does he ride? Make sure you know. If his riding skills don't match yours and you are forced to make an emergency stop, that rider will hit you. If you don't fix the situation through clear communication, your complacency will hurt you. (Brian Blades)

Above: The telltale sign of the classic single-bike accident: a skidmark left by the rear tire at the entrance of a corner. The Pace is all about good judgment and controlled straightaway speed to give you a better chance of slowing for the next (potentially tricky) corner. (Dennis Morrison)
Right: Racetracks have runoff room, a predictable environment and an ambulance. The street does not. This rider's intense riding position and cornering speed leave little margin for error and no room for the unexpected. (Jeff Allen)

Get the Racerboys on the racetrack. If you have overly aggressive riders in your group, insist they go to the racetrack to purge their competitiveness. Notice that the word *race* is part of the word *racetrack,* but not part of the word *street.*

LESSONS FROM THE RACETRACK

WATCH FOR WILDNESS Racers quickly learn whom to trust and whom to be wary of. Their lives depend on it. Know whom you can ride close to and whom to stay far away from.

NO SUDDEN MOVES Don't make sudden moves in big groups. On the first lap of a race, when the pack is bunched together, it's unwise to make radical direction changes or speed changes. Be smooth and deliberate in a group. On the street or track, be predictable.

SPEED ALERT A raised left hand or an outstretched leg signals a slow rider on the track because there are no turn signals or brake lights. This type of communication is vital, and street riders should use flashing brake lights, turn signals and even a raised hand to signal a significant lack of speed.

LOOKING AHEAD Racers soon learn to look ahead of the rider they're following. If you stare at the back of the lead rider, you will be constantly surprised. Look ahead of the rider you're following and use your peripheral vision to maintain the lead rider's position.

RIDE YOUR RIDE Many beginning racers talk about being "sucked in" when they try to follow a more experienced, faster rider into a corner. On the track or on the street, ride your own ride according to your skills, motorcycle, tires, intuition, mood and fitness level.

TOTAL FOCUS Total concentration is a universal trademark of all the best racers. Develop your mental skills as you work on your physical riding skills, and know that a lapse in concentration is the primary reason for single-bike accidents on the street or track.

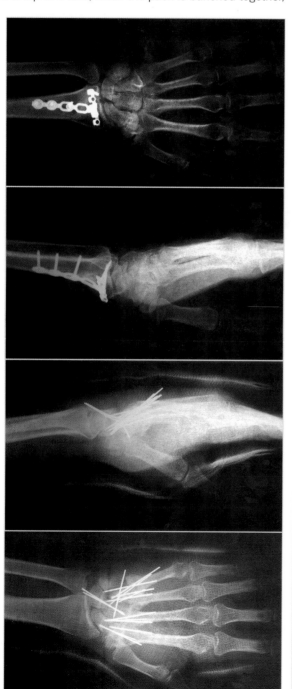

Above: This shot of Eric Bostrom leading a pack of AMA Superbike racers illustrates the ultimate group riding session. These racers depend on consistent and predictable actions from everyone in the group, just like street riders. Surprises hurt any group ride. (Brian J. Nelson)
Left: Ugly reality check. These x-rays are of my friend's badly damaged hands after he was rammed by an oncoming rider who had crossed into his lane. Your number-one rule must be to never cross the centerline, except to pass. The potentially fatal consequences of this mistake underline the importance of controlling your bike's speed and direction at corner entrances.

Right: How can you get hurt sitting still? By not pulling far enough off the road, especially in a right-hand corner. The riders near the white line are putting too much trust in everyday drivers. Get way right. (Brian Blades)

EPILOGUE

Some writers use bold type or italics to emphasize the important aspects of their work, grabbing the reader's eye to make a vital point. If I tried that in this book, most of the words would be bold and italicized, because there are so many critical aspects to this sport that should be emphasized. If I tried to summarize this book I'd simply have to write the whole book again! Just because words you have been reading aren't bold or italicized, don't think they weren't carefully chosen to emphasize my points. All this stuff is important.

Information in this book will affect you in different ways, depending upon your two-wheeled experience. A beginning rider may be much more concerned with mastering emergency braking than picking up the throttle smoothly to load the rear tire. A club racer looking to take the next step in speed may be examining trail-braking and the little things he or she does with the controls. Wherever you are in your riding career, I guarantee you that the things I work on to win an AMA road race are the same things I work on to survive and enjoy the street. Certain techniques work on a motorcycle. Other techniques don't, and they hurt.

Despite my reluctance to summarize the entire book, I will add a quick review of some items riders need to keep foremost in mind. Remember to work with the bike, relaxing and resisting the desire to force, muscle or over-control the motorcycle. Practice correct techniques all the time or you won't have the muscle memory in a true emergency. Dress for the worst-case scenario, because modern riding gear does an amazing job of protecting you when your body hits the asphalt.

Remember that the street is for riding with your friends, the racetrack is for competition. The quicker you ride, the smoother your control inputs must be. Riding when impaired by drugs or alcohol continues to be the main reason motorcyclists crash. Big speed on the street reduces time and distance in an emergency. Avoid blind spots. Don't ride with idiots. Stay totally focused on your riding.

Develop a no-tolerance policy with yourself in terms of riding errors, because "good enough" really isn't. We don't just walk to the net and retrieve the tennis ball in this sport, but the relatively high physical risk is directly related to the incredible feeling motorcycling provides. It's initially addicting and only gets better the farther up the skills ladder you climb.

I felt a social responsibility to write this book because single-bike accidents continue to plague motorcycling, despite the improvement in technology and tires. Riding techniques stuck in the '80s simply don't translate well to modern bikes, and my experience on the street, track, and in schools proved that we are the on-board engineers, and by using the controls correctly, we stay in control. Move your eyes, keep your brain and hands calm, relax on the bike, master the brakes.

It's my hope that you pore over this book, revisiting it often as your experience grows. Any successful person will tell you the same thing: You never stop learning.

Left: A new track and 190 horsepower can be a recipe for disaster without proper riding habits. My guest ride of KRJR's RGv500 at Phillip Island was made easier by ingrained riding techniques that allowed me to deal with all the unknowns. Smooth control inputs, proper body position and good visual habits should remain the same no matter what the environment. (Gold & Goose)

Following page: Jumping from my Yamaha TZ250 to the Honda CBR900RR in 1993 and 1994 taught me so much about approaching the limits of traction on different bikes and different tires. Finding limits is much more survivable by taking many small steps instead of one big leap. (Brian J. Nelson)